The Best of Nature

Terry R. Thomas

Thanks for all you do for nature.
Best Regards,
Jerry Thomas

www.nature-track.com
The Best of Nature, Copyright © November 2013 Terry R. Thomas
All rights reserved. This book is protected under the copyright laws of the United States of America. Any reproduction or unauthorized use of the material herein is prohibited without the express written permission of the author.
ISBN-10:1494300613
ISBN-13-13:9781494300616
Cover Design: Del Moss

DEDICATION

This book is dedicated to everyone who loves and appreciates nature and even those who think they don't.

Copyright 2013

CONTENTS

Contents		v
Acknowledgments		
Introduction		1
Chapter 1	**Musings**	3

    Wandering
    The Between Season
    Sense of Direction
    Questions
    Names
    Leaving Sign
    First Snow
    Seconds Count
    Curiosity
    Making Do
    Morning is the Best Time
    Why I Hate Wolves
    Cairns
    Nature's Engine
    Inner Decay
    This Old Tent
    Beyond Skin Deep
    Thanksgiving
    Lesson From a River
    Cabin Fever
    Outdoor Challenge
    Getting Along
    Collections
    Deadlines

Chapter 2	**Ecology and Biology**	53

    Biomimicry
    Unforgiving Nature
    Who Pooped In the Park?
    Ecological Traps
    Ecological Traps 2
    Spotting Wildlife
    Facing the Wolves

Anthropomorphism
The Trouble with Being Male
The Aster Family
Water: A Wildlife Magnet
Bearpaw Fire
Food Caching
Plundering the Cache
Burrs Under Your Saddle
Animal Communications
The Eyes Have It
China's War on Sparrows
Hoar Frost
Natural Sounds
How Do They Do That?
In Memoriam
Carrying Capacity
Dormancy
It Takes a lot to be Cool
Mountain Weather
Snow Drifts
Good Dads
Winter Tracking

Chapter 3   **Wildlife**   113

Marsh Wrens
Love of Wildlife
Best of the Best
Best of the Best 2
Deer Tales
From Eagles to Gulls
Yellow Jackets Must Die!
Know Thy Enemy
Wild Horses
A Tale of Bears and Wolves
Roaming House Cats
Coots
Wooly Bear Weather Forecasters
Nature's Historians
What's Your Batting Average?
Bats are Essential
Metamorphosis

Snakes Alive!
Chipmunks
Skunks
Drakes in Drag
Dancing with Sharptails
Craneflies
Marks of Autumn
Flying in a Flock
Just a Robin?
Colony Nesting
Insignificance
Ticked Off
Bird Migration
Gray Jays are Yearlong Residents
Feeder Wars

Chapter 4 Places and Times   179
The South Fork
Exploring Close to Home
Iowa isn't Idaho but—Surprise!—it isn't Hell Either
Lake Bonneville Flood
No Wasted Moments
Decisions
New Places
April is a Month of Renewal
New Places Equal New Critters
Mount Everest Virtual Tour
Camping on Public Land
Mountain Lakes
Bosque Del Apache

Chapter 5 People Outdoors   207
People We have Met
Smart Phone Apps for Nature
Essentials
Darby Girls Camp
Fifty Ways to Learn from Nature
Street names
Religion on the River
Teaching Kids about Nature
Backyard Habitat
One Hundred Ways to Die

| Chapter 6 | **Last Word** | 229 |

Bloom Where You're Planted

| **About the Author** | 233 |
| **Readers Write...** | 234 |

ACKNOWLEDGMENTS

I want to thank the many readers who, over the years, have sent me emails, responded to columns via the Post Register website, or told me personally that they enjoyed a specific nature column or the column in general. Nothing has helped me persevere through the tough times more than your kind words and the hope that my own words might encourage us to take better care of the natural world.

I thank Post Register Managing Editor, Rob Thornberry, for his sometimes painfully candid assessments of my writing and his insistence on keeping the writing "tight". It has been challenging, but has made me a better writer and hopefully, provided you with better copy.

I am indebted to my daughter, Elizabeth Zufelt, and my sister, Pamela Christy, for their editing skills and the time they devoted to this work even though their own lives were impossibly busy. It is a far better product because of their comments, critiques, and knowledge of the written word.

I would like to thank Del Moss for his tireless efforts in designing the cover for this book. His talent and skill are apparent and appreciated.

Most of all, I thank my wife, Cathy, for her unflagging support. She has been my greatest fan and cheerleader, and my partner on adventures and exploration. Many column topic ideas were hers as she buoyed me up when my well was dry. She carefully proof-read each column and this book many times, and provided difficult to hear feedback essential to improving both. I know now that it was no easier for her to say it than it was for me to hear it, but she had the courage to do it anyway. This book, and indeed, the column itself, would not have been possible without her.

INTRODUCTION

On page 51 of this book, I describe the challenges I have faced when writing a weekly nature column for the past 16 years. While there is no end to the subject matter that nature provides, finding the right subject at the right time can be a tremendous ordeal.

I have always strived to write about things that are relevant, stimulating, and useful to you, the readers. I have written from the soapbox, looked for lessons in the ordinary experiences of life, and championed wildlife of all kinds, always searching for something positive, even in such seemingly offensive creatures as skunks and yellow jacket wasps (well, I didn't look very hard on that last one). At times, I felt that what I needed to say could put me in hot water with my employer or my peers and sometimes I said it anyway. But, it is still seldom easy to decide what to write about and when.

If there is anything in my life for which I was destined to do or be, it is this: an observer and commentator of nature and wild country. There is no finer calling in my mind. That there is someone who might enjoy my musings is the icing that makes the cake a dream come true.

The selected stories span the life of this nature column to date. Some are personal favorites of mine; others seemed to strike a chord with readers. Some have an important message or lesson that perhaps will resonate with you. My goal has been, and continues to be, to simultaneously entertain and educate about the wonderful workings of nature. I hope at least one story makes you laugh out loud and another one brings a tear to the eye and warms your heart. I especially hope that readers will finish the book and feel a renewed or expanded sense of appreciation for nature and a desire to better care for it. If all that truly happens, then I will have succeeded well beyond merely selling books.

I have meticulously edited these columns and have found faux pas ranging from errant punctuation to colossal and embarrassing errors in syntax, logic, and form. Also, free from the constraints of a 500 word column, I have edited content, adding here and there for clarification, additional interest, or just for my own literary satisfaction. I think I have created an improved product. I hope you will agree.

We struggled with whether to leave the columns reflective of the time that they were written in or to update them to mirror our current situation. For instance, over the course of years, our lives have moved from a house full of teen and pre-teen kids to an empty nest where grandkids come to play. Should I update the column about camping with kids to reflect that or leave it as it was written? For the most part, I chose the latter, preferring only to update when there was good reason, such as significantly new information, to do so. Otherwise, all the writing would be retrospective, not that of someone living in the trenches, so to speak. You may sometimes see a progression in attitudes and philosophies, perhaps even contradictions, as life experience and time have helped to mold and shape my viewpoint.

I hope you enjoy this first volume of, *The Best of Nature*.

CHAPTER ONE

MUSINGS

Wandering

My erratic path through the woods would have been puzzling to an observer. I veered left here, followed an elk trail there, scrambled on top of rocks, skirted one deadfall, and fought my way through the next. In the course of several hours, I had wandered toward every point of the compass—completely random, with only inquisitiveness to guide me.

My wandering wasn't without purpose, though. I had come here with senses dulled from dragging them on the concrete of city life—I needed to hone them back to, well, if not a keen edge, something sharper than a marble.

I chose to wander rather than to hike. Hiking has a clearly measured objective: to reach the destination, hike a certain distance, or even to garner the benefits of exercise. A good hike or even a brisk walk to clear the head can achieve these and still allow the hiker to devote brain power to solving problems back at home or the office.

Wandering is aimless, has no pace, and adapts and meanders as interesting things catch the eye or tantalize the ear or even the nose. It has no tangible measure of success; but to be successfully done, wandering requires abandoning civilized cares and focusing on whatever stimulates the senses.

The Apaches say that every place has its own wisdom and to learn that wisdom you must be in that place. That is the only objective in wandering: to see as deeply into the workings of the place as possible and to learn the wisdom there. If there is a motto for wandering, it is simply, "Wherever You Are, Be There."

Two questions guide a wanderer: *Why?* and, *What is this?* This search for answers usually leads to more questions—and more questions, not answers, are often the result. It is childlike, not childish, movement, finding wonder in the ordinary and cherishing each minute.

Re-lighting the candle of childlike curiosity is not a simple task, especially when the wick has been cut short by constipated adult attitudes and "real life". Indeed, it was more difficult than I had imagined, this letting go of my modern world. It was much like asking a turtle to shed its shell. I realized I felt vulnerable and naked without my anxieties. What if they actually weren't important?

As I wandered, I tried to engage all my senses. I sniffed the air like an Aborigine, and found it heavy with pine scent and perfumed with the occasional bouquet of elk. I listened to absorb every sound; what did I hear and what was missing? I touched the coarse pine grass and ran my fingers along the deep furrows of the Douglas firs. I wanted to notice every detail, feel a belonging, and become more than a visitor.

There were two extra payoffs that day: the first was a fox den, situated on the crest of the hill. Abandoned this late in the season, it is someplace to revisit in the spring. The other was an elk skull, white with age but with broad five-point antlers still attached. Neither could be found along a trail and both added dimension and wonder to the day.

I recommend wandering, even if you find it difficult at first to shed the burdens of your life. You will discover intricate workings, intriguing treasures, and perhaps observe wildlife behaviors that those who stick to trails may never witness. Most of all, you might re-discover the child in you, and in today's world, that is a treasure worth more than gold.

The Between Season

A season exists between winter and spring that, being neither one nor the other, leaves me impatient and anxious. Winter reluctantly relinquishes its grip as rotting snow recedes in jerks and spurts, closing the door on many winter activities and leaving a void in the world.

Spring fights for a toehold, but the portal to summer is still locked. It's a season of muddy days and frosted nights, a season where, in many places, "you just can't get there from here."

The between season isn't recognized on the calendar. Officially, spring has been here for a week now, and as I write this, a beautiful vernal day is waning. I have seen enough springs, though, that while I am cheered by a warm day, I am not fooled. It would be no surprise at all to awaken to a world blanketed once again in white. March may come in like a lion and leave that way, too.

This is the teasing season as winter and spring swirl together and wrestle for dominance—hope and despair are inseparable partners. Today I saw my first box elder bug, yet the snow shovel is still in its place on the porch. Days are lengthening, beckoning me to be outside, but the wind still has a bite that rasps my throat and morning temperatures plunge into the teens. The surface of the garden on the north side of the yard is muddy and slick, but beneath, the frozen ground is shovel-bending hard.

Spring will win. I know that, and its supremacy is even now becoming apparent as winter was particularly weak this year. Snow is still piled in the shady places, but where the grass has been relieved of its cover it is slowly awakening.

New guests are arriving at the bird feeders to avail themselves of my hospitality, a sure sign that winter is on the way out. House finches, red-winged blackbirds, and the inevitable house sparrows flit through the yard and drain the feeders daily. I can walk through drier parts of the yard and not track mud back into the house. Where frost has faded, backyard tulips are poking through, in an apparent race to beat the front-yard crocuses still locked under piles of snow shoveled from the walkway.

In the marsh, geese wander about, waddling across ice, honking their impatience to get on with the business of spring. The ice that supports my weight in the morning is mushy, soft, and treacherous in the afternoon.

A trip north to Island Park demonstrates that the full dress of winter isn't far away. By St. Anthony, the ground is once again white. Several feet of crusty snow still trap Island Park in winter's chill. But deep wells around each tree testify that even here, winter's iron grip is slipping.

There are those who, desperate to prolong winter activities, will follow that snow like Bedouins, hoping for one last chance to play. But even the high country will succumb to the between season, as winter becomes increasingly furtive. The days fast approach where the deep snow will rot into a patchwork and travel by snowmobile, ski, or even on foot, becomes an impossible challenge.

The between season seems to have so little to offer that sometimes I feel like an alien in my own backyard during this tumultuous time. What am I supposed to be doing? I cast about, like a bird dog that has lost the scent, looking for the best opportunity, that one thing the season offers that I shouldn't miss, but it is like a dream where I can't find my other shoe.

It finally dawns on me that perhaps this restlessness, the wandering and poking my nose into old haunts, pushing to find spring, is the reason for the between season. It is about taking the time for reconnection and reawakening, and once again finding my reflection in nature.

Sense of Direction

I have been lost in the woods, sometimes hopelessly lost, more times than I care to count. Partly it stems from my penchant for off-trail exploration, but mostly I confess to absolutely no sense of direction. I know people who have an almost supernatural ability to navigate in the darkest of jungles and emerge EXACTLY where they wanted to go or, even more amazing, find their way back to where they started. Not me. No matter how many times I turn around and check out the back trail on the trip in, the return trip seems like it is in a different mountain range.

I lay the blame for my inability to tell direction directly at the feet of my upbringing. You see, I was raised in Salt Lake City, a city where streets run either north and south or east and west. It is a city perfectly and properly organized with the terrain as well: the big mountains lie to the east and the little mountains to the west, and both flank the valley in perfect north/south lines. Growing up there, I had little need to actually tell direction; it was already done for me.

And that is how I subconsciously believe the world is organized and when it isn't, I get lost. To this day, when I am confused (which is much more frequently that I would normally admit to) I still have to close my eyes and orient my surroundings in reference to my mental image of Salt Lake City.

This can be a serious handicap. When I lived on the Clearwater River, the woods were thick and dark. There wasn't any place where you could get a perspective on the country—the next hundred yards looked just like the last and ridges ran in all directions. For a guy used to the wide open spaces of the sagebrush desert, it was like hiking into the Brazilian rainforest. At night. Getting oriented, mental image of my hometown notwithstanding, was impossible. It took a long time before I ventured far enough to lose sight of the road without pockets stuffed with the modern equivalent of bread crumbs: flagging ribbon.

Actually, often I am not lost, but rather, I tend to misplace something such as my truck or camp. I know that the road is at the bottom of the hill, but when I get there, do I go right or left?

Because of my affliction, for much of my life, I rarely saw the purpose of a compass. What good does it do me to know where north is if I don't know which direction I want to go? On the other hand, my Global Position System (GPS) unit is invaluable and has saved my legs on a number of occasions. It guides me unerringly back to my truck well after dark and puts me back in camp before the dinner dishes are put away. And it makes the compass a far more useful tool: if the GPS says to go south, I can use the compass to tell me which direction that is.

But, even technology lets you down. Just last week, my GPS unit told me that I was headed 90 degrees in the wrong direction. No amount of tapping or re-booting would convince it of its error, so in frustration I finally turned it off and continued on with my internal compass. Hey, I only missed my destination by just under a mile.

I try to look on the bright side, though. I have seen a lot of country while wandering around hopelessly lost, and to date, no one has ever had to call out the search dogs to find me. If that ever happens, I am confident they will find me sitting on a log where I will nonchalantly ask, "Say, have you fellows seen my truck?"

Questions

Mount Katahdin is the highest point in the state of Maine and, depending on whether you are heading north or south, the beginning, or end of the Appalachian Trail. It is famous for at least one other thing: in 1908 the last native woodland caribou to leave a track in Maine soil was reportedly spotted on its slopes. As a species, caribou had already been extinguished from neighboring states of New York, Vermont, and New Hampshire, as far back as 100 years previous. Caribou then quietly slipped away from Katahdin slopes and a place where they were once so numerous that Caribou, Maine, was named in their honor.

But the woodland caribou was still abundant in Minnesota, Michigan, Idaho, Montana, and Washington, so the loss was hardly noted. Gone from Wisconsin by 1850, these other states slowly followed suit until by 1955, the population in the Selkirk Mountains of northern Idaho and eastern Washington was the last of the U.S. segment of a species that had once been abundant along most of the 3500 mile border with Canada.

Even in Idaho, the range of the caribou shrank like a tired balloon. Caribou once wandered in the Clearwater River country and provided sustenance to Native Americans and hungry pioneers alike. But logging, fires, and unregulated hunting all took their toll until only the Selkirk population remained.

Despite years on the Endangered Species list, $4.7 million spent on recovery, and the translocation of over 100 animals, woodland caribou in the United States barely hang on. In fact, some local residents believe that within the continental United States, woodland caribou are functionally extinct—those we see are just wanderers from the British Columbian population. They argue that it is time to stop recovery efforts, especially the proposed designation of 375,000 acres as critical habitat for woodland caribou.

The concern is that the critical habitat designation will restrict recreation, timber harvest, livestock grazing, and the rest of the gamut of competitive human uses of the same area.

And so, unsettling questions are raised. For instance, does there come a point where recovery efforts for a species should be abandoned? If so, what is the measure for that? There are good examples of heroic recovery efforts that have kept species on this planet. California condors and black-footed ferrets come to mind. Is their recovery worth the cost?

Another challenging question asks: What is the worth of a species and how do you determine it? I used to think that this question was answered in 1973 when the Endangered Species Act was passed, but we seem to still continue the debate. Does it all come down to economics? If so, how do you determine the economic worth of something whose value is not understood or even comprehensible? How do you put a price on something that pays not in cash but in serenity? How do you calculate the worth of foregone scientific advances that a species may have offered in the future? How do we know if the inconveniences, lost revenue opportunities, and restrictions inherent with species recovery are worth it?

The thought that inconvenience is justification for extinction is disquieting—if we can justify extinguishing a species because it interferes with profit or pleasure, what else, with just a little more motivation, will we be able to justify?

After woodland caribou disappeared from Maine, two subsequent reintroductions failed. So, as we strive to answer these questions, one fact remains: once a species is gone, it is gone and extinction is a heavy word. We should weigh that fact carefully.

Names

In our ordered world, everything has to have a name. From the tiniest microbe to mountains and streams, we aren't satisfied until they are properly identified, classified, categorized, and named.

In the case of living things, the scientific name is relative to its family tree. Mountains, rivers and other geographic features are often named for their discoverer or some benefactor.

It makes you wonder then, how the names that refer to groups of animals came about. Why is a group of cormorants, those fish eating birds, called a *Gulp*? We understand what a *Pack* of wolves means, but, what about a *Dule* of doves?

Sometimes, these names make some sense. What else would you call a gathering of buzzards if not a *Wake*? When two or more porcupines are united you couldn't help but call them a *Prickle*. And clearly, a group of finches is not just a mere flock, it is a *Charm*, while gathered larks are an *Exaltation*. When sapsuckers band together they could be nothing less than a *Slurp* and a congregation of rhinos is obviously a *Crash*.

Occasionally, group names depict our relationship to, or opinion of, the creatures so named. An assembly of wise owls is called a *Parliament*. A swarm of mosquitoes is called a *Scourge*, and a group of gnats is called a *Cloud*. A cluster of otters is a *Romp* and a crowd of leopards is a *Leap*. Borrowing from the Old Testament, a group of locusts could be known as nothing else but a *Plague*.

There are also times when a grouping has several names depending on what the group is doing. A bunch of pheasants on the ground is a boring *Nide*. However, when they flush, they become, fittingly, a *Bouquet*. Swans are in a *Bevy* until they line out in a V pattern. Then they are a *Wedge*. Wolves lazing around are a *Pack*, but on the chase they are a *Rout*. Geese on the ground are a *Gaggle*, in the air a *Skein*. It is a *Raft* of ducks on the water but a *Flock* in flight. And for fish, it depends on if they are alive, a *School* (or *Shoal*), or dead in a creel, a *Mess*.

It is apparent however, when names were being thought of, creativity was not always the order of the day. For example, groups of such diverse species as ants, beavers, penguins, and bats are all *Colonies*. Bittern, heron, and crane reunions are all *Sedges*. And, we understand that a group of large mammals such as deer, moose, antelope, or bison is a *Herd* (however, elk hang out in *Gangs*).

Some group names make no sense at all. Why are multiple bears called a *Sloth*? A sloth is not a bear. Why are hordes of flies called a *Business* and bees called a *Grist*? A group of foxes is a *Leash* and frogs en masse is an *Army*—foxes on a leash? Armies of frogs? I don't think so. These names seem to be victims of imaginations in overdrive but not necessarily connected to reality.

Some of my favorites are in the corvid family. What will you call the next gathering of magpies? A *Tiding*, of course. Ravens congregate in an *Unkindness*. And crows are obviously Hitchcock fans (*The Birds*) because when they unite they are a *Murder*.

For our family though, it was the *Mustering* of storks last Thursday that had the most meaning to us. A granddaughter came into this world, and for the sake of order, was promptly named Zoe Elizabeth--a name I will always love.

Leaving Sign

There is a game that I play whenever I traipse through remote country that goes something like this: *I wonder if I am the first human to step here, see this particular rock or tree formation*, etc. The actual realization of this game is one my of my greatest fantasies.

When my sons and I scrambled up peak 11,272 in the White Clouds this past summer, I was deep into this fantasy. It was a rugged climb and served no purpose other than to say we had done it and to witness an incredible view. Maybe, just maybe, we were the first with such noble and pointless ambition. At the top though, the log book tucked in a Mason jar pulverized the fantasy.

It appeared that this un-named peak in the middle of nowhere should have had traffic lights on it. Not counting the entire scout troop that had summited, there were at least a dozen other people who had enjoyed the view in just the last two years. Even our difficult route was routine.

I began to doubt, once again, that there is any place left in this country where one can truly even foster the illusion of being the first person there. Exploration of a true Lewis and Clark nature, even on a minute scale, seems to be dead. Each time I think I have found IT, a candy wrapper, boot print, or a name scratched on a rock or carved in a tree dashes my fantasy like a stone crushes glass.

I can readily think of some steep talus slopes and cliffs that likely have never felt a human's weight, so I suppose my lament is tinged with laziness. But even there, a wind-lodged scrap of paper or a tired helium balloon from a far away birthday party could easily dash the illusion just the same.

Leaving something to mark our passage and to ensure that others know that they are not the first seems to be an almost primal urge. I have read cached journals from the top of Mt. Borah, to Peak 11,272, to Bald Mountain in the Wind Rivers. I have even seen the brass plate firmly drilled into the rock on top of the Grand Teton. And, although I find these artifacts fascinating and enjoyable, I might be able to revel in my fantasy, but for these reminders.

I have my own inconsistencies too. A name carved into a tree significantly before my birth fascinates me. The discovery of a now crumbling cabin or mineshaft in some remote canyon nearly equals the thrill of first exploration. Finding a heretofore undiscovered petroglyph would be Nirvana itself.

I reconcile myself to the fact that my boot will likely never fall on virgin soil. But if I can't be first, the discovery is still new for me.

I have a new game now, one that builds on the old one. I pattern it after the conservation slogan, *Leave No Trace*. At the end of the day, wilderness is found as much in the mind and heart as on the land. With my new game, wilderness and its promise of new discovery is preserved if the next explorer never senses I've been there. And, I hope for the same from others.

First Snow

Muzzleloading rifle in hand, I ventured into woods transformed into paradise by six inches of fresh snow that frosted trees and ground. More was falling, and it was so still I could almost hear the snowflakes settle on the branches. It was a tracking snow and exactly what I had been waiting for.

Just steps away from the truck and I was swallowed up in primeval forest and immersed in the experience: primitive weapon in hand, eyes scanning for elk tracks in fresh snow, looking for a shadow of movement, out to feed my family from the bounty of the land.

The snow continued to fall, covering my hat and cotton jacket like natural camouflage. Cotton. What a greenhorn. I was in such a hurry to get out and hunt in the snow that I was ill-prepared for the event. I hoped I wouldn't pay dearly for leaving the woolies home.

The surroundings were so mesmerizing that elk hunting quickly became secondary. I marveled at how clean, fresh, and new the snow made these woods that I thought I knew intimately. Familiar sites looked novel and different, mysterious, needing exploration. "Why hadn't I seen that tree before?" " Look how the snow makes that burnt stump look like a bear."

The trees around me bore their charming snow load stoically. Occasionally, the burden would become too much, though. A branch would sag, releasing the snow in a puff, like smoke from my muzzleloader. I couldn't resist kicking the trunk of a Christmas-sized tree just to see the snow fly. November snow brings out the kid in me.

Silence and stillness embraced the woods in a slow dance. Even the lightest snowflakes fluttered straight to the ground. There wasn't even a hint of breeze to carry my human scent to the elk. The silence was so powerful my heartbeat, hastened by the hike and the excitement of the hunt, sounded like a drum I was sure even the elk could hear.

Once, a raven broke the silence, "Caw, caw, caw." It was so incongruous, so out of place in the stillness, that it startled me. But I welcomed the distraction as it woke me from my reverie. Moments later, with a whoosh of raven wings and a final caw, the pleasant quiet descended again. I dusted fluffy snowflakes from my jacket and hat and picked up the hunt again.

I found elk tracks and followed. Some tracks were filled with snow. But three sets were fresh. The perfect setup. I was in a race with the setting sun, though, and I was hurrying to catch up. Five steps...look instead of one step...look. Moving too fast is always a mistake.

When the elk appeared, they were like apparitions. One second nothing, the next, there they were, looking at me, the only moving thing in the forest. Their nostrils flared and clouds of steamy breath exploded as they trotted soundlessly off. Busted. Again. Oh well. The day was worth it.

Beautiful. Silent. Still. Perfect. The first snows of November mark the change of seasons in splendor equal to autumn's glory. For those of us who may not really relish cold weather, November snows, with their mystical beauty, offer a flawless and gentle transition into the dark cold of winter where snow can become a worrisome burden.

Seconds Count

As the sun rose at Florida's Ding Darling National Wildlife Refuge, photographers stood hoping to capture one second of action when a brown pelican launched itself into the air. We watched as he waddled near a sandbar about 30 yards away. When he sprang from the water, it seemed a laborious process to get that big body airborne. Even so, shooting at four frames per second, he was completely airborne in five frames.

In our society, we seem to take seconds for granted, wasting them like pennies. When I can slice one second into four distinct moments though, it is amazing to see the detail a second can hold. I shouldn't find that surprising. My own heart, despite years of exercise, still pounds out 70 beats every minute, more than one per second. That alone should make me a respecter of seconds.

The value of a second is well illustrated in nature. For a rattlesnake, a second is plenty long enough to carefully aim, execute, and recover from a strike. Twice. In that time, it opens its mouth, unfolds its fangs, lunges, bites and injects venom, then folds its fangs back again, closes its gaping mouth, and returns to a coiled up position. That is a lot in half a second. Even then, the strike portion is only 0.2 seconds long.

The hummingbird is an animal that knows the value of a second. Hummingbird wings beat so fast that there isn't a camera around that can capture them. To stop a hummingbird's wings requires a burst from an electronic flash unit that can produce a flash duration as short as 1/50,000 of a second. That is because a hummingbird's wings beat a full figure eight pattern at the incredible rate of 50-100 times per second. In comparison, if I really try, I can blink my eyes about five times per second.

And for hummers, that is just the beginning. Their hearts beat 21 times a second. And, even though they are not exceptionally fast fliers, they can cover 40 feet a second. Not bad for a creature that weighs a tenth of an ounce.

Larger species also understand the value of a second. Pheasant hunters won't be surprised to learn that a flushing rooster can put 88 feet, nearly 30 yards, between himself and the hunter in one second. A pronghorn antelope can do the same, and can keep it up for miles. A white-tailed deer is slow in comparison, covering only 51 feet per second, about three car lengths, in an all out sprint.

Bighorn sheep rams start their head-butting fights from about 35 feet apart. They rear up on hind legs, running forward several steps before dropping to all four feet and finishing their charge with a thunderous clashing of heads. All in two-fifths of one second. With the fastest motordrive, a photographer is lucky to get one frame of the peak action.

In nature, seconds do matter. Life, death, and procreation can all hinge on even a slice of one second. That might be where wise old Ben Franklin got his inspiration when he penned, "If thou dost love life, then don't squander time. For time is the stuff life is made of."

Curiosity

I doubt I have ever seen more classical natural behavior than when my wife, Cathy, and I were photographing a blue grouse in Yellowstone Park. But it had nothing to do with the grouse. We were just 30 yards above the Beaver Pond trail, which begins and ends at Mammoth, when a group of teenagers came into view. Cathy counted them as they passed by and she finally gasped, "104 kids!" Not a single one saw us—each trudged along the trail head down, oblivious to our presence despite Cathy's red jacket. Uninterested in the beauty all around them, they were present, but they really weren't there. I suspect their un-inquisitive minds had already raced forward to the buses they had arrived on, to television, music, and friends— archetypal teen behavior.

Of all the skills related to the serious study of the natural world, possibly the most important is not an education, but rather, the development of a resounding sense of curiosity. We discovered the blue grouse because Cathy heard an unusual noise (a male blue grouse looking for a love interest makes a call somewhat similar to the hoot of an owl) and slowed my own headlong, head-down march until I heard it too.

I suspect that more can be observed and discovered through simply learning to apply the questions, *"Why...?"*, *"Why not...?"*, *"What is...?"* or *"How does...?"* than any other technique. It is the surest way I know of keeping the senses—senses that are quickly dulled by city life—vigilant, focused, and working in unison and it is probably the basis for all scientific discoveries and advances. And you don't have to be a scientist to practice it—anyone can do it.

If you want to learn how to ask questions, follow a child into the woods. Children are masters at probing questions. And they usually don't stop at a single question. Each answer we give is followed by another inquiry, usually simply, *"Why?"* A child bares the essence of nature like peeling an onion. Each question builds on the next, probing deeper and deeper.

This incessant questioning can drive a curiosity-constipated adult bonkers. I sometimes wonder at that. After all, it is perfectly acceptable to wonder why butterflies have wings or why fish don't have legs. It is possible that we have wondered the same things (or worse, we have never speculated on them) and lack of a suitable answer unsettles us. What if they ask something even more profound?

For the inquisitive, everything is an adventure. Many a hunt has been salvaged when curiosity compelled me, much like the chicken, to push to the top of the hill just to see the other side, or around the next bend in the trail simply because I have never been there. Unpretentious observation of any rock, leaf or track can lead to a question that leads to dozens of more questions and the beginning of true understanding.

So, look up, peer down, peek inside—change your perspective and see the world from a different angle and ask yourself what you see, why it is there, what it was, and what it might become. Embrace the mystery, search out the answers when you return home. And remember, for the most part, the most important thing is not the answer, but the process of stimulating your curiosity enough to ask the question in the first place.

Making Do

In the Craig Thomas Visitor Center at Moose in Grand Teton National Park, I listened to the woman in front of me as I waited to get a boating permit. With a Georgia accent she complained to the information ranger about the paucity of wildlife. "We drove all the way through Yellowstone," she grumbled in a soft southern drawl, "and all we saw were a couple of deer." The ranger told her where she might see elk and bison, but the woman walked away with the ranger's comment ringing in her ears: "They are wild animals though, and unpredictable."

I grinned inside, a touch arrogant because I had a plan that was sure to yield big game up close and personal. Cathy and I would float from Jackson Lake Dam to Pacific Creek and play around at Oxbow Bend. This area is surefire for big game and I was prepared with two cameras, extra memory cards, and a gut full of anticipation.

The float started out well. A bull elk bugled from the base of Signal Mountain and it sounded like he was moving closer to the water's edge. But the bugling faded and no elk appeared. So we looked for moose. On two different occasions, moose have crossed this area right in front of our canoe. On another, a huge bull stood patiently while I photographed him and his lady friend against a number of intriguing backgrounds.

But not today. Even though two more elk teased us with bugles from a distance, mammals of any sort were not to be seen.

As I thought about that Southern Belle at the visitor center, my arrogance faded and I commiserated with her plight. Two thousand or even two hundred miles to visit Yellowstone or Grand Teton National Park is a long way to drive only to have the abundant big game be all coy and shy when you get there.

I busied myself with other photos, though. We lucked upon a common snipe hunkered down and trying to go unnoticed on the shore. This proved to Cathy that the long ago girls camp hunts for mythical snipes were not so farfetched. A couple of ravens were way more tolerant than usual and a hen mallard posed as if she were a paid model.

Then there was the dragonfly. She was so intent on mating that I could literally reach out and touch her. Even though the breeze rocked her perch like a cradle, she was still there when I left after finally capturing a few blur free frames.

A bald eagle, mergansers, and an osprey or two rounded out the day and left me in a conundrum. I did not even see a big game animal, the subject of my effort, yet I made some pretty nice images. So, my quandary: was the trip a failure or a success? A pessimist would argue that since the object of my visit was unsatisfied, the trip was a failure, regardless of whatever lemonade I managed to make. Failure is failure.

But Cathy is an optimist and argues that my portfolio is brimming with elk photos. However, dragonflies, snipe, and osprey with freshly caught trout are images of which I am decidedly lacking.

It reminds me that in life, you don't always get what you want. Sometimes, what you get is better.

Morning Is the Best Time

When the alarm sounded last Saturday at 4:00 A.M., I should have bounced excitedly out of bed. But, I'm not a morning person, and getting up early, even to go hunting or, in this case, to photograph a new sage-grouse lek, is a challenge. I wrestled with conscience and the snooze button several times before dragging myself from beneath the covers.

I missed the turnoff to the lek in the darkness but finally found it using GPS coordinates. By then, though, the sky was orange and I was too late to get into position for a photograph. So, I enjoyed a stunning sun rise, watched the sage-grouse strut from a distance and listened to horned larks sing in the crisp spring air.

When that show faded, I headed to Market Lake Wildlife Management Area. At 9:00 A.M., I saw hundreds of birds and a lone long-tailed weasel, but not another human. For most, the weekend hadn't even begun, yet my day was already awesome.

Morning. Without a doubt, it is the best time of day to see wildlife and appreciate nature and life itself. Morning begins well before the sun rises, when the day is still just a promise etched in a blush of pink and orange against the eastern skyline. This is an enchanted time when nature's daily rhythm begins to rev, contrasting against stillness and solitude.

Solitude is the first thing a novice to the wee hours might notice. For those immersed from rising to retiring in the daily hubbub, the morning stillness and solitude initially might be unsettling. But, soon, early morning solitude lifts the burden of daily distraction from the shoulders. Senses numbed by the buzz of city life are revitalized, and really seeing and hearing become a joy once again.

Morning solitude can be found just about anywhere, because so few actually avail themselves of it. Even a crowded summer day in Yellowstone National Park is an adventure in quiet solitude in the early morning hours.

Then there is the light. Even before the sun inches over the horizon, the sky is filled with orange and pink and red, and shades of purple ride on the clouds. As the sun rises, everything is bathed in a warm light that photographers cherish. The low angle of the light unveils and accentuates detail that is subdued later in the day. There is a beauty there that fans my internal spark into a flame like no other time.

There is no better time to see wildlife than the break of day. Deer and elk wander from feeding areas to bedding areas. The song of the lark, the wren, and other birds can be heard best in the clear still air before wind and background noise rise up to squelch and subdue them. Geese lift off with a roar and head out to feed. Sage-grouse dance, elk bugle, and sandhill cranes call in the morning hours.

During the short winter days, I see sunrise through my windshield on my way to work. During the summer months though, mornings begin early enough to take advantage of it before "real" life starts. If I can't get away to a place like Market Lake, a walk in my yard will do. I look for butterflies and birds, and measure the progress of my garden. Mostly though, I am looking for serenity. I always find it and that makes getting out of bed early worthwhile.

Why I Hate Wolves

I hate wolves. It is good to get that off my chest. I hate them, but probably not for reasons you might think. Wolves have become a distraction; something that has kept our focus centered on what will ultimately turn out to be a small, no, miniscule issue in the grand scheme of conservation over the next 50 years. We are spending our precious time and resources agonizing over trivia and ignoring the tsunami that is bearing down on us.

Wolves, ducks, elk, wolverines. These are all merely actors on the stage of habitat and their populations will ebb and flow in response to habitat quality and quantity regardless of our best arguments. When it comes to long-term conservation though, where should the emphasis be? Should we focus on the actors or preserving the stage?

Last week I attended the annual conference of the Idaho Chapter of the Wildlife Society. The theme of the conference was the future of wildlife 50 years from now. Wow. I will likely be dead by then. In that sense it won't matter to me. But my grandchildren will be my current age. Will they curse my name for not preserving for them the natural world I loved and enjoyed?

An eastward glance at the windtowers on the Idaho Falls skyline tells us that the world around us is changing and changing rapidly. That was one message from the conference; the juggernaut of change is racing toward us like a runaway train. Here are a few things we can expect in the next 50 years:

- As climate changes, spring run-off may decline by an average of 50%. There will still be relatively good years but there will also be many more drier years and more moisture will come as rain rather than snow—one result of which is that reservoirs may not fill and springs may go dry.
- Over the past 100 years, species ranges have shifted northward about 61 kilometers and the pace will accelerate. Habitat is disappearing for species such as the woodland caribou. It already barely exists in the United States at the very southern tip of its range and further northern shifting of that range in response to climate could push caribou north out of this country. Other species will face shrinking habitats as well.
- Idaho's population is expected to double in the next 40 years. With growing populations come increased demands for living space, water,

energy and recreation, all of which will place untold demands on already limited resources. Without smart-growth planning, helter-skelter development will permanently impact many of the things Idahoans cherish.

- The number of species endangered by regional, national and global changes will rapidly increase and we will to be forced to make some very challenging triage decisions. These challenges are already evident: the sage-grouse and the wolverine have both been warranted but precluded from listing under the Endangered Species Act because of higher priorities.

All of these threats, and whatever new ecosystem threats our lifestyle creates, make the wolf-eats-elk argument seem petty indeed. Yet, the papers are full of stories about litigation, legislative bills, and outraged citizenry on both sides of the wolf issue vehemently arguing for their point.

There isn't one word though, on the changes that are coming that will nullify all these arguments if those changes aren't directed, deflected or deflated while they still can be. One day we may look back with considerable regret that we allowed trivial arguments to derail us from far more significant problems that will demand all of our collective creativity to resolve.

Cairns

Pack straps chafed at my shoulders and sweat dripped from the end of my nose as I stared at the giant boulders and wondered how to get across. The woodland trail I was following had ended abruptly in an intimidating rockslide and there was no alternate route: the slide ran far up the hill and the terminus had its feet wet in a soggy meadow thick with willow and bog. I cautiously stepped onto the first boulder and looked for my next move.

With a heavy pack, I didn't want to make a misstep. I jumped from boulder to boulder several times, but realized my wife would not be able to do the same. She'll go anywhere there is a trail, but crossing this boulder field would be a test beyond measure. It was my job to find a better way.

Then I saw it: to my left, half a dozen rocks stacked to precisely form a small tower. Twenty yards beyond was another, and then another. Trail cairns, stones stacked high in a pyramid shape, marked a way across the treacherous slide to safety beyond. Relieved, I changed course to get on track with the cairns and waited for Cathy. Together we easily followed the cairn-marked path through the maze of rocks. As long as we kept the cairns lined up, the otherwise obscure route unraveled like a rolling twine ball.

I thought about another time when cairns marked the way. Once again, a fine trail we were following faded in a meadow. The trail was unsanctioned and we expected some cross-country work. Following the creek up to the lake seemed reasonable. Before long though, our mistake became obvious. The dog whined, terrified as we shouldered 60 pounds of quivering golden retriever up over cliffs and around ledges slick with algae. When we reached our goal, we were scraped and bloodied, exhausted from an arduous and dangerous climb. We were also anxious about the trip back. Some of the scrambling would be much more difficult when reversed.

We didn't notice the cairns at first. The path we were scouting didn't look measurably better than our path on the way up. But someone had been there before and had taken the time to mark an easier and safer way. The first carefully placed pile of stones was a welcome surprise. We changed course when we spotted it and confidently marched from cairn to cairn until we reached the meadow. The cairns took out the guesswork and provided a way down even the dog could appreciate.

More than just a haphazard pile of rocks, trail cairns are carefully placed to designate the way through an untracked wilderness. The trail maker may have wrestled with cliff edges and bogs, crevices, boulders, and slippery scree, backtracks and dead ends, but the final trail reveals none of it. Each carefully stacked cairn points safely to the next, circumventing the hazards as much as possible as long as the follower has the faith to travel the unmarked ground between them.

Metaphorically, our life's path is lined with cairns. Ramblings, deviations and digressions, unsure or misguided steps need not leave lasting marks in the hard rock of life. The decisions we make—to have a family, to finish school, to right a wrong, to accept responsibility for the world around us—these are the marks we leave behind, the stones from which our cairns are built. They are lasting tributes and show the way for those who follow.

Nature's Engine

I don't know if my sons remember it, but I do. We were at a fair somewhere, and the most fascinating display was a car engine made of transparent plastic. All the parts moved exactly the way they would in a real engine. We could see each component and how it worked with the rest of the engine, all in intricate detail. Pistons moved up and down in perfect order and drove the crankshaft at the bottom of the engine. Valves opened and closed, dancing with the cams, and precisely timed to the exact position of the pistons. The distributor meted out spark exactly where it needed to be and when it needed to be there. All of this worked in perfect unison, each part exactly serving its function and doing it flawlessly.

It was clear that this complex machine had to be finely regulated in order for it to work properly. If a spark plug failed, it would still run, but the efficiency and smoothness would disappear. If a part were to break, it could wreak havoc on the entire motor.

Fast forward to a couple of years ago. I was moving snow with a blade attached to my lawn tractor. Without warning, a clattering noise had me reaching for the key to shut the machine down. It was too late. The engine died on its own, never to start again. A growing pool of oil forming in the snow as it dripped from a jagged hole at the bottom of the engine told the story. I immediately thought about that clear plastic motor and could envision what had happened.

Two bolts held the piston arm to the crankshaft. One of them had likely given way and with the piston descending under explosive force, it was only a matter of time before the second bolt fractured. Then, with nothing to hold the piston arm to the crank, the arm drove through the bottom of the engine with the energy of a jackhammer.

One single part failed inside this complex machine. Its failure was undetectable until, catastrophically, it manifested itself and caused the demise of the entire engine. It could have been any number of parts though—worn rings, a broken oil pump, a blown radiator hose—any of these could have caused the engine to fail in a big way.

The lawn tractor debacle wasn't my fault, but I admit that my own tinkering over the years has caused more than a few of my own troubles. I know just enough about cars and engines to be really and truly dangerous to my own self interest. I have put parts in backward, reversed wires, installed spark plug wires in the wrong order, mounted the wrong parts (hey, that wasn't always my fault), and too often, ended up with far too many spare parts at the end of a job. When it was all said and done, I probably caused more damage than I fixed, because I thought I knew what I was doing and I was too cheap to pay to have it fixed professionally.

It isn't farfetched to take this engine analogy and apply it to a vastly more complex system: Nature. In our attempts to have it all, we trivialize natural processes, pretending we understand them well enough to mimic them, replace them, or ignore them if we must. We remove pieces from a finely tuned system assuming they were never needed in the first place, break others and presume that it won't matter. When science highlights our follies, predicting calamities that may arise from our arrogance, we decry the science as flawed, or worse, that it is science with an agenda. When the natural engine fails, we point fingers, wondering who forgot to check the oil.

We should remember one thing: in the long view, we are far better off to maintain the engine than to try and fix it after it has thrown a rod. At that point it may be too late, and we will have to face the consequences.

Inner Decay

Even on a hillside full of giants, the Douglas fir tree at my feet was monstrous. Two men reaching around its base wouldn't touch finger tips and it stretched out along the ground for over one hundred feet.

I had heard the terrifying sound of large trees falling on this mountain in the past, but when this one crashed down it likely made them seem trifling. The impact must have shaken the ground for hundreds of feet in all directions and hurled out bark and splinters like shrapnel.

When it fell, nothing in its path was spared. Limbs on neighboring trees were sheared off down their lengths, leaving them lopsided and open to disease. Smaller trees, directly underneath the fall line, snapped in two or had roots ripped from the ground as they were flattened.

The trunk did not yield easily and the sapwood around the base was a shattered mess. Huge dagger-like splinters jutted up from the trunk. Large fragments of bark and wood had exploded out from the rupture line as if dynamite had been placed inside. On impact, the rough bark on this behemoth—thick, strong, and excellent insulation against fire—had peeled off in huge slabs. One massive chunk of sapwood had been ripped out from the windward side and created a hole so large I could step into the center of the tree.

What had finally brought this veteran of hundreds of years to the ground? Certainly, with a crown higher than the other trees, this giant stood alone against the unmitigated forces of the wind. Eventually, the relentless mountain winds had brought the leviathan down. But was the wind the cause or just the agent?

The real cause of the giant's demise became apparent when I looked at the core of the tree. I picked up a handful of heartwood and easily crushed it in my hands. White fungus had been attacking the tree for years. Although the outermost wood was solid, the heartwood and adjacent sapwood were rotten and did not lend support to the rest of the tree.

The decay hadn't happened overnight. White fungus rot moves slowly, perhaps just centimeters per year, so infection could have begun before the first fur trappers were investigating the Henry's Fork. But the fungus methodically and inexorably chipped away at the inner strength of the tree until what remained couldn't support it.

I stepped back from the center and carefully examined the outside of the tree. Based on appearances, I would never have guessed at the weakness within. I pulled hard at a jagged upright piece that held fast to the root. It was solid and strong. I dug at the wood with my knife and quickly decided that was a job for better armed woodpeckers. To a layman forester like me, there were just no obvious outward evidences of the disease that cankered the heart of this great tree.

When I walked away from that tree, I realized that Nature had presented me with a life lesson. Age is slowly catching up with me on the outside, but, am I also slowly rotting at the core? What small sores, habits, and thoughts am I allowing to fester that could one day be my undoing? I think I need to look through the window of my soul to see what condition my heartwood is in.

This Old Tent

Over the last few years we slowly transitioned from tent to trailer camping, a evolution in life I didn't think I would ever embrace. But the kids have left the house and trailering is so convenient, fast, and comfortable for middle aged campers. And, let's face it, camping in bear country, especially where there is a food storage order, has changed the face of camping. Elaborate tent camping kitchens are a thing of the past when everything must be locked away whenever camp is unoccupied. Trailers make sense.

That wasn't always the case for our family though. I uncovered my old tent in the garage the other day and hefted it, catching the scent of canvas. With the aroma, memories engulfed me like the rising surf.

I purchased this tent over 25 years ago with the proceeds from the first two articles I sold to *Field and Stream* magazine. For over twenty years, it was part of almost every family vacation, hunting, fishing, and photography trip. Tent camping taught my kids to be self-reliant and responsible campers, not ones dependent on all the comforts of home when camping.

This tent's fabric is the guardian of memories of trips to places like Island Park, Meadow Lake, Glacier National Park, Wildhorse, Yellowstone, and Pittsburgh Landing, salmon fishing at Riggins, and camping in 20 below zero while hunting deer. We spent hundreds of nights in that tent with our kids; telling stories, playing games, and reading aloud books such as, *Mysterious Island, My Side of the Mountain, Swiss Family Robinson,* and other tales that had captured my own imagination as a youth.

The fabric also carries the marks of two decades with stories to match. There are long tears where a bull elk raked his antlers against it in Mammoth Campground in Yellowstone. Sixty-mile-an-hour Wyoming winds once flattened the tent and bent some poles, but I replaced one and fixed the other and it was good as new. And there was the occasional abuse such as the time when, chainsaw in hand, I tried to remove a hazard tree and instead dropped it right across the tent. A missing grommet and a few rips and separations are from wear alone, but there are surprisingly few, given that five rambunctious kids and several dogs grew up within its walls. Careful drying and cleaning has kept mildew at bay and the tent is still ready for use at a moment's notice.

This particular tent is not one of the sissy lightweight nylon tents of today, the ones that set up with the flick of a wrist. No, this tent is not complete without five large bags and enough stakes to stabilize a circus big top. It is huge, heavy, and rock solid, perfect for a family. Better yet, set up isn't intuitive, making it a poor loaner tent.

As I held that bag in my hands, I felt the melancholy guilt that comes from abandoning an old friend. This tent had been the key to hundreds of happy days afield, had been integral in raising my children with a love for nature, and I had shamelessly left it behind just for the sake of convenience.

I wonder if trailering has truly improved my camping experience or if getting back to my roots, to my old friend, is really better than expediency. I think I'll take that old tent out for another trip. Maybe there is still a place for both in my car camping life.

Beyond Skin Deep

On my desk is a dry stick plucked from a sagebrush skeleton while hiking through the desert. I was in no particular hurry when I picked it up, so I sat on a lichen covered lava outcrop and idly pulled out my pocket knife. Like a kid, I whittled on the stick, my blade making one lazy pass, then another through the rough twisted surface as I absently thought about other things. The wood carved easily—it was not mushy, just not hard like oak. The pile of shavings grew quickly and I glanced at my handiwork. It wasn't just a stick of sagebrush anymore. Beneath that gray and rugged exterior, inspiring only thoughts of a fragrant fire, a rich light brown wood with an intriguing grain emerged. My whittling was the only blemish and I started to carve with more care, smoothing and trimming.

Over several weeks I have been polishing this carving with sandpaper so fine there is no apparent grit. It has become far smoother than I anticipated it could be and the carved portion is taking on a deep gloss, almost an inner glow. It is the perfect foil for the remainder of the piece that remains in original condition, a yin and yang of wood, the natural versus the potential.

When I showed my wife my handiwork, she was amazed. "That's sagebrush?" she questioned. "I didn't know it had a beautiful wood grain like that." Indeed, it is a work of art that was waiting to be unveiled.

In furniture, we call the wood lines grain, but they are really growth rings, an annual record of life for this branch. I count 13; several wide ones, depicting years of plenty, followed or preceded by very narrow bands, indicators of drought or other stresses, a reminder that life is capricious— good years and lean years are inevitable and there is no sure way to predict either.

Each time I work on my carving the beauty grows and I wonder if, with enough buffing, it will become like the gleaming stones in my son's rock collection. Ordinary stones these, but when subjected to the constant action of fine grit and polish in a rock tumbler, they slowly transform into smooth polished bits of glass. Gone are the rough edges, the coarse textures and imperfections. Ordinary stones, yes, but with enough polishing they unveil unimagined beauty and are so clear that they glow in a beam of light revealing even more inner detail.

One aqua blue rock in particular boldly shows that once the veneer is stripped away, even rocks may be built one layer of sedimentation at a time.

Like the growth rings on my carving, on this rock there are fat layers when sediments ran with plentiful spring rains and thin ones when drought plagued the ancient land.

I turn back to my stick and twirl it slowly in my hands. I run my fingers over it, admiring both the smooth carving and the rough twists of the native piece. There isn't a right or wrong side here, but there is a lesson: what we see on the outside may have very little relation to another beauty that is deep within, just waiting to be uncovered and polished with care.

Thanksgiving

There are over 718 flowering plants, 80 species of mammals, 89 birds, 40 reptiles, 25 amphibians, and 138 fishes listed as endangered or threatened in the United States. Habitat shrinks by the day as subdivisions, resorts, and other developments vie for the same ground as wildlife. Climate change, energy developments, dams, West Nile Virus and chronic wasting disease, pollution, drought, water wars, and invasive species all grab for headlines. Political machinations conspire to strangle agencies into submission to political will rather than science.

With assaults on nature coming from every side, it is no wonder conservationists are a pessimistic, glass half-empty bunch. It seems their lot to fret over innumerable threats to our environment. Is the glass ever half full? Each day is spent parrying with existing threats and bracing against new ones. It seems that Aldo Leopold was right when he penned, "To have an environmental education is to live in a world of wounds."

But once in awhile, we need to step back and remember the victories. We all need to look around and appreciate what we have, if for no other reason than to strengthen our resolve to continue the fight to maintain a nation vibrant with the influence of the natural world.

For instance, a glass half-empty conservationist might bemoan the fact that dams impede salmon and steelhead migrations on the Snake River. A thankful conservationist would realize that without long pitched battles, four additional dams would have corked the Snake River between Hells Canyon Dam and Lower Granite Dam and likely would have been a death blow to anadromous fish.

A glass half-empty conservationist chafes at the large number of species threatened with extinction. A thankful conservationist will remember, from time to time, that conservation works—as witnessed by the revival of white-tailed deer, wild turkeys, and elk, all severely reduced at the turn of the 20th Century and now abundant nationwide. Bison came from the very brink of extinction to become well established in wild herds and in several national parks. And there is more good news: 20 species, including the American Peregrine falcon, American alligator, and the bald eagle have been de-listed from the Endangered Species Act as recovered.

A glass half-empty conservationist recoils at the amount of habitat lost each day. A thankful conservationist will recognize that our nation likely has a higher percentage of real estate protected in National Parks and Monuments, wilderness areas, wildlife refuges, and public land in the form of National Forests and BLM properties than any nation in the world.

A farm bill, active since 1985, has protected tens of millions more acres of private lands, improving wildlife habitat and reducing erosion. Millions of more acres of private lands have been protected by conservation easements through the diligent efforts of land trusts and dedicated landowners.

A battle weary conservationist might despair, thinking that the war is being fought by an outnumbered and outgunned minority of similar minds. A thankful conservationist will recognize that public support for conservation has never been higher. Organizations such as Pheasants Forever, The Nature Conservancy, Rocky Mountain Elk Foundation, Land Trusts, Mule Deer Foundation, Ducks Unlimited, Trout Unlimited, Master Naturalists, and more are teeming with volunteers who dedicate their time and money toward furthering the cause of conservation.

The struggle to maintain our natural heritage is far from over. Progress has been real, though, and we should all be thankful for what we have and for those who fight to make it so—all of us.

Lesson from a River

From its dual beginnings at the foot of Yellowstone National Park, Wyoming and Island Park, Idaho, the mighty Snake River winds in a convoluted path. The North Fork (or Henry's Fork) weaves its way south out of Island Park, plunging off the caldera lip in a series of waterfalls: Sheep, Upper Mesa, and Lower Mesa Falls.

The South Fork reports to work at Jackson Lake in Grand Teton National Park and then flows west where it again punches a time clock at Palisades Reservoir. Spilling through the dam turbines it rumbles northwest through Swan Valley.

From Swan Valley, the river sweeps north to join the North Fork at Menan, ricocheting off the volcanic glass of the twin Menan Buttes that were once its riverbed. The co-joined rivers course south through Idaho Falls, punching the time clock again at Gem Lake and American Falls Reservoir before turning and meandering west across southern Idaho. With a gradual turn north it spins turbines at four more dams before, after a long sinuous journey, it bends west again, entering Washington State and meandering toward its destiny as part of the Columbia River.

If the river could have run straight from its origins to Clarkston, Washington, hundreds of miles of twisting rough and tumble travel would have been avoided and the Snake River would have a different name. But mountains stood in the way. The Palisades, Bitterroot, Lemhi and Centennial ranges and more forced the river to find an easier, if more circuitous way.

The current footprint of the Snake River is not its historic course. The river is alive, a wandering minstrel across the valleys and plains through time. In some places, to be sure, it is captive between walls of black basalt or deep canyons. Once, the river wandered through these areas too, but with time, and with the help of the floodwaters from the breaching of Lake Bonneville, it cut downward and became trapped. Now, with surging waves, it rages against its captors but it is forever chained in these deep canyons.

Within the gentler terrain of the valleys and plains though, the river has always danced, as it inevitably overcame all resistance to its awesome power. Through ages, the river meandered around the valleys, twisting and turning to avoid high ground and circumvent obstacles. It is never content—if there is an easier way it will find it, using spring floods like a battering ram against resistance.

It deposited evidence of these ancient wanderings: deep gravel beds full of smooth round stones, thick sand bars, and sloughs mark primeval channels. Quiet, isolated oxbows mark where the river more recently flowed and where it may want to flow again someday.

From its origins in high mountain streams to its meandering path—first south, then west, then north, then west again—the Snake River knows only one rule: follow the path of least resistance. It can never oppose the pull of gravity and run uphill. It constantly probes for weaknesses and abandons the old course and adopts an easier one without remorse. Always seeking the easiest path, the Snake River serpentines across Idaho, earning its name.

There is a lesson in the Snake River: it became twisted and crooked by following the path of least resistance. People are the same. And, eventually, like the river, we become trapped by our choices. Our potential is liberated only when we struggle against the odds, intentionally choose the upslope climb and fight against the temptation of the easy, but crooked, way.

Cabin Fever

Cabin Fever. Restlessness or anxiousness induced by prolonged exposure to inside activity, usually caused by unrelenting winter, without appropriate stimulus from Nature.

That's my definition and last Saturday I had it bad. In desperation, I visited the Snake River Greenbelt and practiced photographing ducks and geese in flight. My fingers numbed and the birds settled down way too soon, though, and I was reduced to aimlessly wandering.

I ventured into several home improvement stores checking out all the gardening materials beginning to grace the shelves. I tried to visualize my yard, but I couldn't even muster a mere illusion of green. Spending green from my wallet on landscaping left me hollow.

My daughter, a registered dietician, would have chastised me severely when I tried to drown my sorrows with a burger and a shake but I didn't care. The world was out of sync. March seemed like January and summer too distant to imagine.

Then my son called. Returning from Jackson, he had seen a large group of mountain goats nearly on the highway just upriver from Alpine. I couldn't believe it. "Goats?", I asked. "Are you sure?" Exasperated, he described them as white fluffy things. Goats for sure.

Even high gas prices couldn't hold me back. I have often commented about how difficult it is to see mountain goats and I wasn't going to miss my chance to observe some easy ones.

In less than two hours I was a few miles east of Alpine Junction parked just inside the white line on Highway 89, alternating camera and binoculars against my face.

The goats had moved back up the hill and were resting and feeding on the south face of a rocky outcrop about 200 yards away. While this wasn't exactly "almost on the highway" like my son had seen, it was still quite a show. They were easy to spot against the gray rock. In all, I was able to count 30 goats.

I observed that they were more an off-white than snow white. Regardless, when viewed without binoculars, their winter camouflage was incredible. On those gray cliffs, they appeared to be lumps of snow.

A sheriff's deputy stopped to ask if I was all right. I replied that I was just watching the goats. He nodded understandingly and moved on.

Most cars zipped past even though it was obvious I was watching something on the hill. A few stopped and looked too, but most pushed on, anxious to get to their destinations. Likely these goats had been here all winter and these folks had already stopped a hundred times to admire them.

A nasty thought kept popping up though—what if they just don't care? Could it be that an opportunity that had lured me away from home, a chance to see a rare sight like a mountain goat, just isn't as important as the errands of the day? If our lives are so busy we stop taking an interest in the marvels of nature, an elemental connection of our wellbeing will break. What will that mean for society?

As I drove the 80 miles back home, I forgot the ill wind that had wafted through my mind and my spirits ran high. Just seeing a bunch of mountain goats had banished cabin fever like a giant natural tonic.

Outdoor Challenge

A friend of mine loves to run trails. Before he moved north, one of his favorite runs was Teton Canyon. His group would run from the trailhead, through Alaska Basin, over Hurricane Pass, and end up somewhere near Jenny Lake, a distance of about 20 miles. After that got too easy, they began making it a round trip, all in one day, carrying only little packages of stuff called "Gu" for sustenance and a bottle or two of water.

I can only wonder what it must be like to be in that kind of physical condition and I have the utmost respect and admiration for my dedicated friend. I hiked that trail on Saturday and didn't quite make it to Alaska Basin. I returned to the car bone-tired, aching, blistered, and craving a Pepsi.

I know power hikers for whom a good day on the trail is measured by two things: reaching an objective and doing so in record time. I met two such hikers a couple of years ago on the trail to Green Lake in North Leigh Creek. I could see them well below me and before long they were passing me. They spent less than 20 minutes at the lake before heading back. I spent four hours and regretted leaving.

I think about some of the outdoor competitions I have heard about: for instance, bagging all of Idaho's 12,000 foot peaks (itself an awesome lifetime achievement for anyone) in the shortest time possible. The record time for climbing all nine? A blistering 28 hours and 50 minutes.

Or how about bagging all California's 15 or Colorado's 54 14,000- foot peaks? Or running the Grand Canyon rim to rim and back (called the R2R2R)? It is only a distance of 45 miles but with 10,500 feet of elevation gain. The current record is four seconds shy of seven hours even.

It seems as if humans have completed the domination of the outdoors and nothing is left except the physical challenge of doing more and/or doing it faster.

But it leaves me uneasy. Have our treasured wildernesses and craggy peaks become nothing more than natural gymnasiums? Does taking a day to climb Mt. Borah diminish it as a crowning achievement because someone routinely does it in a few hours?

My treadmill can give me more workout than I can stand. When I come to the wilderness, it isn't for physical challenge or to beat someone else's time, but for connection and renewal, a chance to see wildlife, and experience something rare and extraordinary in my life. I love to bag peaks too, not to prove anything to them or me, but rather to gain from the experience and appreciate the stunning views. Is that different from a race to the top?

On my way toward Alaska Basin, I stopped a dozen times to admire the view, appreciate the incredible wildflowers, to watch a cow moose and her calf, and a red fox. Each pause sliced a little time from my schedule and ultimately I didn't reach the basin. If that had been my main objective, these wonders that made my day would have been sacrificed on the altar of achievement.

These super athletes have convinced me that there is room in my outdoor life for a little more challenge, but I also know that I never want to get so fixated on an objective, a stopwatch, or a technique that I miss the blossoms alongside the trail.

Getting Along

The south end of the National Elk Refuge ends abruptly where it bumps against the homes and businesses of Jackson, Wyoming. At this interface, Flat Creek becomes a spreading marsh as if resisting being sucked into the culvert under the road to be entrapped within unyielding banks of the human domain.

The water is shallow here, perfect for dabbling ducks, but suitable as a stopover for diving ducks and other waterfowl as well. From the wee blue-winged teal to the enormous trumpeter swans, from Canada geese to coots, mallards and redheads, widgeons and ring-necked ducks, and more, the marsh is home for the summer or a billet as they leapfrog between seasonal habitats.

Blackbirds, marsh wrens, and killdeer flit among the bulrush and cattails that line the marsh. This cover is dense, providing plenty of protection from predators and a place to escape harsh weather.

For several hours one blustery day last fall, I watched this avian scene. At first I was a little bored because there seemed to be little action to photograph. I settled in to wait for someone to pick a fight but there was no rancor, no argument, no ill tempers. Nearly a dozen species with obvious differences and they were all getting along. That struck me as odd.

Slowly, I became intrigued. Black coots swam next to the huge white trumpeter swans, sometimes touching them. The swans took no offense. Ducks mingled freely with each other, each quacking in its own language; dabblers swimming with divers, greenheads with redheads, ringnecks with teal. Geese paddled, honked, and tipped up to feed next to the ducks, next to the swans, next to each other. Still no fights erupted, not one single act of aggression.

It even seemed to be more than a lack of enmity. There was cooperation, whether intentional or not. The swans would work their feet back and forth, stirring up the mud before tipping up to feed on whatever they dislodged. Other birds swam in close and took advantage of the muddied waters, dining on what the swans missed, but the swans didn't seem to care. No, "this is mine you can't have it" attitude, it was more like, "share and share alike" without hierarchies or castes.

These birds were different species and sizes, had different mannerisms, voices and languages, yet they were able to get along, completely accepting the presence of others totally unlike themselves.

There are probably a number of boring scientific explanations for a behavior of tolerance but all of them lead to one inescapable conclusion: these birds have figured out how to get along. There were no police keeping the peace, no armies to force cooperation.

Some days, I should look no further than nature to understand many of the lessons that I need to learn to be a successful human being. Here, a mixed group of birds taught me some fundamentals of life: constant bickering saps too much energy. I can relate. All benefit from extra eyes and ears alert for predators. Who couldn't use someone else to, "get their back?" Different isn't bad, it is just different. Maybe I can learn from a unique perspective.

Collections

Wandering in the woods, I happened to notice a few old bones scattered about. Not one to let such valuables go unexplored, I poked around, picking up a femur from under a snowberry bush, digging a portion of a partially buried moldy jawbone from the hard ground. These I inspected, admiring the complexity of the skeletal system, and then set them back down. Further searching netted a real treasure—a vertebra, as large as my hand, weathered but intact. I turned the piece over and over, enthralled by the intricacy of the specimen. Then, like finding an image in the clouds, I discovered an impish "face" staring back at me from the bone. Without hesitation, I stuffed it into my pack to show my kids at home.

Life around our house is often like show-and-tell in school. It is not unusual at all to find a quart-sized canning jar on the counter covered with a lid made from a sandwich bag poked full of air holes, and containing anything from a "cool" cat-face spider, or a praying mantis, to an "awesome" butterfly. Inanimate objects, such as pieces of obsidian, leaves, flowers, feathers or just about anything else can appear like magic on our kitchen table. It is not always the kids who bring things home either. My wife has had to tolerate years with a freezer full of road-killed snakes and other critters that I eventually make into study skins or other "useful" items (still want to eat at my house?).

Collecting natural things is a wonderful hobby, one that can be shared with family members and used to encourage children to understand and respect nature. Our own kids have literally grown up with many of the things I have collected over the years and can talk as intelligently about owl pellets as they can algebra.

So what do you collect and where do you find "it?" That is the beauty of this hobby! Any hike, stroll, or picnic becomes, as the military would say, a "target-rich environment" where there are no limits to the interesting things you can find. Some of the things I have found and treasured include:

- A huge cottonwood leaf—just a network of veins after a winter of decomposition. I still vow that I will make an award-winning photograph of it one day.
- Owl pellets, a personal favorite. These are oblong pellets, one to three inches long, comprised of fur and bone, which an owl regurgitates.

The biologist in me likes to dissect the pellets to see what victims the owls have been eating and the kids love to help.

- Skulls of various animals and birds. I enjoy comparing them to each other and using my field guides to identify the species (even if I already know it). This is another huge hit with kids. (Might as well say it here though: without a collecting permit, you are not allowed to possess any parts of some protected animals such as hawks, song birds or endangered species.)
- Live critters such as spiders, garter snakes, frogs, salamanders, etc. These often have become photographic subjects but my rule is to release them alive in suitable habitat when I am finished. Guaranteed to attract kids so be careful.
- Bits and pieces of interesting geology. These have included a glittering stone from a creek, a chip of red obsidian, a small piece of pumice so light it floats, and a rock that resembles a honeycomb. Be aware though, taking anything, even rocks, from National Parks/Monuments is a major *no no*.
- Anything that says an animal has been there such as a snake skin, bits of fur, feathers, or bone.
- Insects. During my college days, I was required to make an insect collection. It was the most pleasant assignment I have ever had. Cathy, and our son, Jacob, then two years old, would spend afternoons searching the gardens and hills around Utah State University and every new specimen would bring a gleeful, "Dadda, muhh!" ("muhh" meant bug), from Jacob. Since then, I have rarely pinned an insect, but I have captured many, preferring to observe their lives for a little time before releasing them.

I even enjoy rediscovering treasures I have packed away in the odd shoebox or a remote corner of my desk. Each Halloween, for example, I "rediscover" the vertebrae "gargoyle," as it has become one of our favorite Halloween decorations. It hangs on our front door to silently greet visitors.

If collecting nature's odds and ends is an addiction, by all means get hooked. You will find the windows of the natural world will open a little wider for you and offer up glimpses and insights you never knew existed.

Deadlines

There are likely no lonelier hours for a writer than those just prior to a deadline with no firm ideas for the next column in mind. A tsunami of panic, inadequacy, and fear rolls in, and without a lifeline, the waves can deal a crushing blow.

Such is tonight. With less than 12 hours to the deadline for this column, my fingers are impatiently waiting for direction from my brain. My brain is wishing my fingers would stop being so lazy and begin to move without being directed for every keystroke. Worse, unlike many writers, my wordsmithing takes a decided turn for the worse about 11 p.m. so in reality, I have just a few hours left.

After 15 years as a nature columnist, could I be running dry on material to write about? In fact, one of the questions I am most frequently asked is, "how do you keep coming up with all those article ideas?"

That isn't the problem at all. The natural world is so full of the fascinating, the wonderful and the strange, all the nature writers on earth can never do it justice. There are thousands of scientific journals, each reporting research discoveries and ideas in their own area of expertise, topics that would delight the average citizen, even the average scientist. My own list of potential subject matter is pages long, and the clutter on my desk is full of one-line notes with other potential themes. I add to it virtually every day.

And the internet has made my job vastly easier. Gone are the tedious visits to the library, where just searching for a single article could take hours. Research is now all so wonderful, interesting, exciting, and accessible, it is often a challenge to stay on task.

I sometimes get so involved in the research that the writing suffers. I strive for accuracy and am careful to check sources and look for counter viewpoints, but in reality, I am often caught up in a fascination with what I am learning, leaving little time to write. Learning continues to be a personally rewarding aspect of this column.

Tonight I have followed no less than four different topics trying to decide on this week's column. But, I realized they all needed time to gel before I attempt to put them on paper. One of those has been partially written for several weeks and I'm still not comfortable with its form or its substance so I put it aside again, knowing that desperation is seldom a good bedfellow for inspiration.

Sometimes it is not that I am at a loss for a topic, but rather, the subject is so colossal or multi-facetted it becomes nearly impossible to sort and sift and find the nuggets that can/should be highlighted in a mere 500 words. Nature topics are often this way. Which direction should I go? How do I boil down a complex and important subject like habitat fragmentation and get people to care? Often, after I hit the send key I feel I have missed the mark and spend the week wishing I had a second chance.

Sadly, inspiration is often what I lack and inspiration comes from time in the field. With more time in the field, inner vision clears, ideas develop and insights flash into my soul like lightning. But time in the field has been lacking lately and I feel the heaviness that comes from clouded vision. Thoughts are murky and hard to correctly discern. Research, fancy words, and a list of potential topics a mile long are of little use when inspiration fails.

But something has to come together once each week, and bringing it together is the challenge. Dang those deadlines!

CHAPTER TWO

ECOLOGY AND BIOLOGY

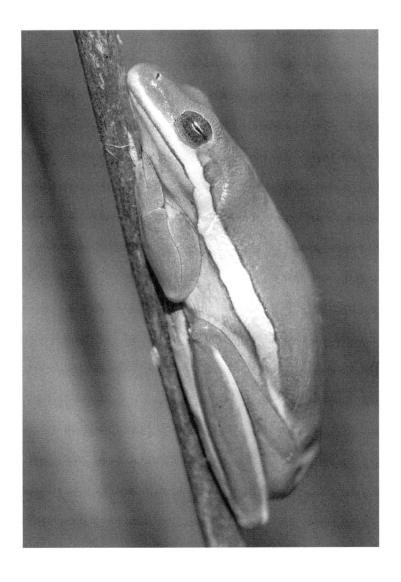

Biomimicry

"*Look deep, deep into nature*, and then you will understand everything better.*" --Albert Einstein.*

I looked deeply at the seashell I held in my hand. Smooth as glass on the inside and somewhat rough but beautiful on the outside, it fascinated me, but I didn't understand it. I turned it over and over, ran my fingers along the protrusions and along the linear-textured growth stripes, wondering what secrets it held, what genius in its creation was yet to be discovered.

It was large, as seashells go-- the fat spiraled end nearly as broad as my palm and seven inches from spiral to the tapered end that curled tight like a scroll. It felt strong and solid and I decided to test it. I placed the shell on a cement floor and gingerly lowered a 20 pound steel weight onto it. No problem. Thirty pounds, then 40, then 45. Not even a squeak of protest.

I fondled the shell again. Here was a simple creature that, through ages of field testing, had perfected a way to create a super-strong home. It constructed it with materials readily available in seawater, without toxic chemicals, carbon footprints the size of dinosaurs, or waste. Amazing. What else could it do that creatures with opposable thumbs have yet to figure out?

That is the thinking at the core of a new science: biomimicry. It is based on the premise that life on this planet has already cooked up solutions to virtually all our human perplexities—we just need to learn how to read the recipes.

Biomimetists study Nature's models, such as the seashell, and then, "emulate these designs, forms, processes, systems, and strategies to solve human problems—sustainably" (AskNature.org). Biomimetists are Nature's apprentices who, when faced with a challenge ask, *How would nature solve this?*

This makes a lot of sense. Earth's 30 million or so species have had billions of years to solve problems. Those that couldn't adapt and find solutions, faded from the scene. We are now surrounded by the whiz kids that developed ways to thrive in virtually any type of environment. And they have done it while taking care of the place their offspring will call home.

Within the natural world are the answers to how to solve just about any issue humans have. Need to de-salinate seawater? Study the mangrove or the sea turtle. Both have very effective ways to do just that. Need a better way to allocate Internet server resources that respond to changes in user demand? Study and apply honeybee foraging strategies. Need a material that will be waterproof and stronger than ceramic but flexible and lightweight? Study how Nature creates mother of pearl from seawater. Want to make a wind tower more efficient? Ask a humpback whale about the scalloped edges of its flippers.

With eons of field testing, Nature has solved so many of the issues we now face. Technology can now unravel the recipes, sort of like reverse engineering, from the creative genius around us. When we allow Nature to teach us how to solve problems, we are well on our way to sustainable living. And that is a dang good argument for zealously protecting this planet's biodiversity: they may yet prove to be the salvation of our species.

For a fascinating presentation on how Nature can help us solve challenges, view Janine Banyu's presentations at:

http://asknature.org/article/view/videos

Unforgiving Nature

In Rocky Mountain National Park, I happened upon a graphic reminder that the natural world is not as idyllic as we might suppose. In the waning light of evening, bull elk escorted their harems out into the open meadows. Challengers were everywhere and eternal, exhausting vigilance was the price the best bulls paid to ensure their genes would be well-represented in next year's calf crop. Several bulls squared off with young hopefuls, but as the light failed me, no serious fighting had begun.

The next morning told a different tale. Driving past the same meadow, I noticed an out of place lump. It was an elk, a modest sized bull. His pierced body was evidence that the posturing the night before was, to the bulls, very serious indeed. Whether he was a challenger that let his lust out-weigh his judgment or an exhausted harem bull that made a mistake in battle, I don't know. But the lesson was clear: Nature is a hard task master under the best of conditions.

When snow piles up on winter ranges, cold temperatures reign and food is in short supply for most big game animals. Natural selection begins to call the weaker animals home. That is to be expected and is healthy for a herd of say, mule deer. That way weaker animals are constantly being culled from the gene pool and adaptation to new circumstances continues (if humans lived under this regime, I suspect I would have been culled long ago!).

But nature is challenging all the time to wildlife, not just during winter. Animals are not immune to accidents or even just plain bad luck.

Research conducted in the Lochsa River country in north-central Idaho, revealed that 14 out of every 100 elk deaths were attributable to accidents. A few years ago, I harvested a cow elk and found a half inch diameter, 18 inch long stick embedded between her right shoulder and her ribcage. On an "effortless" run through the forest she had impaled herself. A few inches further left and she would have become a different kind of statistic.

Some animals, like mountain sheep and mountain goats, also live in country that is inherently dangerous. My graduate school professor told me about his search for a missing radio-collared ram. The radio-collar was equipped with a mortality sensor that told him that the ram was likely dead. But that was the perplexing part. Standing in the middle of a rockslide, the receiver indicated that the signal was close, but there was no carcass. When he stepped back, he tripped over an exposed horn. The rest of the animal was buried under the rockslide.

Another radio-collared ram in Oregon disappeared after a storm in the high country it called home. That autumn, he and three other rams were discovered—all victims of a lightning strike.

Mountain lions live incredibly dangerous lives. Not only do they haunt high rugged terrain, but they jump on the backs of animals weighing up to four to five times their own weight and often sporting an impressive array of antlers or horns. Dr. Maurice Hornocker, who conducted classic research on Idaho lions in the 1970's, wrote that young lions were, "injured more frequently than has been believed." Researchers in Utah once encountered a lion skull with a piece of mountain mahogany piercing the brain cavity. They postulated that the cat had attacked and had run into the branch, killing it instantly.

Avalanches, rockslides, lightning, goring, impalement, falls, windblown trees, fence entanglement, quagmires, and wandering off cliffs (100 antelope did this in Wyoming in 1944) all take their toll on wildlife populations. Biologists call this additive mortality—deaths that add to whatever other causes are operating on the population (i.e., a smaller or larger population would not likely change the natural accident rate). It is not likely that the impact is significant to most populations, but it shows that even wild animals mis-step, mis-calculate, or are just in the wrong place at the wrong time with tragic consequences.

That fact ought to make city dwelling, pavement pounding humans doubly cautious when venturing into the wilds. If accidents can happen to animals that spend their lives dealing with the elements, we are certainly vulnerable to mishaps as well.

Who Pooped in the Park?

While on a hike in Yellowstone, my wife and I met a couple of young brothers, Clue and Les, from Illinois. After giving them some directions the conversation turned to bears. Clue, the elder brother, stated that they didn't want to go back the way they came because of all the bear scat they had encountered on the trail. I was perplexed and taken aback—I, a trained professional, had missed something so obvious?

My wife caught on first--"Oh, you mean the bison dung!"

With a wipe of his brow, Clue declared, "Whew, I'm glad it wasn't bear! I was really worried". Les just stood there, oblivious to everything.

It has become obvious that scat identification may not be as commonsensical as I had presumed. After our experience with Clue and Les, my wife confided that in her younger days she thought deer pellets were pine nuts. On a trip to southern Utah with a friend, she thought she had found pine nut heaven until she tried to break off the shell. Surprise!

Despite the stories, this is a serious article. In fact, while in the Park, we found a children's book entitled, *Who Pooped in the Park?* giving evidence that others think this is a legitimate scientific topic as well.

Scat (the pseudo-scientific term for the proper but gross sounding word, feces) or droppings identification is as important as track identification for unraveling animal tales on the ground. Not only will scat tell you what animal you are dealing with but will also tell you who is eating whom. You really have to know your $%@! to get into poking through poop (and I include owl pellets when I refer to scat, even though they are regurgitated and not excreted) but it can make you feel like a real naturalist.

Here are the basics of scatology. Let's start with the big guys. Bison are roughly the size of cattle and eat similar diets, so it stands to reason that buffalo dung looks an awful lot like cow pies: a big, green, generally shapeless mound. Often, though, bison dung is drier and tends to form large layered lumps. Either one works fine for a nice fire when completely dry.

Moose, elk, mule and white-tailed deer, mountain sheep, mountain goats, and pronghorn antelope have similar droppings. The oblong pellets resemble well, pine nuts, except the scat is usually in piles and pine nuts aren't. Within species, there is considerable variation in pellet shape and size, due to diet and age of the animal. For instance, when these species are feeding on succulent vegetation, pellets may be much softer and drop in clumps instead of individual pellets, and youngsters have smaller droppings than adults.

Telling moose from elk from deer scat is mostly a matter of size. Moose pellets may be the diameter of a man's thumb and up to one and a half inches long. Pellet groups are also larger: a single moose may deposit a quart or more of pellets at one time. Elk pellets are similar but smaller than moose, usually half to one inch long, and larger than deer pellets which tend to be only about three-eighths to half inch in diameter.

Rabbits and hares also have pellet like droppings ranging from less than a quarter inch to half an inch in diameter. These pellets are usually more round than ungulate pellets but can occasionally be confused with droppings of fawn deer.

Predators such as wolves, coyotes, foxes, bears, and mountain lions tend to have ropelike excretions full of such things as hair, insect parts, porcupine quills, and other indigestible matter. Bears and coyotes are particularly opportunistic feeders and in season their scat may be full of grass, berries, or seeds.

With these predators, there are species-specific differences, but size is a main indicator. Wolf dung is far larger than coyote while a grizzly bear is the top pile-maker of them all.

Finally, of course, the question that everyone really wants answered is how to tell black bear scat from grizzly bear scat. That is easy: Black bear poop is full of grass and seeds. Grizzly poop is full of hiker warning bells and whistles and smells like pepper spray!

Resources: A good field guide is essential for any budding scatologist. I recommend: *Mammal Tracks and Sign* by Mark Elbroch, *Scats and Tracks of the Rocky Mountains*, by James Halfpenny and, *Animal Tracks, a Peterson Field Guide,* by Olaus J. Murie. This last one is a classic.

Ecological Traps

As a young boy, I spent a week each summer on my grandfather's farm in Springville, Utah. Aside from hunting corncrib mice and cherry-robbing starlings, and snooping through my grandfather's shop full of interesting rusty metal parts, I helped with haying. A ten-year-old city kid really wasn't much help, but I rode the tractor with Grandpa while he mowed the hayfield. He used a sickle mower that operated with scissor-like blades, much like a modern hair trimmer. As we worked around the field, nesting hen pheasants hunkered down, hoping we would pass over their nests. The sickle bar was set just a few inches above the ground though, so at the last moment, the hens would stand and the sickle bar would remove their feet, condemning them and their nest. My job was to exit the tractor on Grandpa's command and try and catch the hen for supper. A few footless hens made it to the table, but most escaped—they could still fly—to become a coyote or fox's next meal.

Theoretically, animals select habitats where they can successfully reproduce and stay alive. Like the pheasant hens, though, sometimes they can be fooled by habitat that appears superior but ultimately "traps" them with some unseen and unanticipated future event or condition.

Ecological traps have the illusion of high quality that becomes a fatal attraction or results in lost production. Indeed, alfalfa is excellent nesting cover and, when managed for pheasant, can produce a lot of birds. But harvested during nesting season, this great habitat suddenly springs the trap. Other ground nesting birds are affected too. Research shows that a wide variety of songbirds prefer to nest in alfalfa but have lower nesting success there than in native habitats.

Ecological trap theory in conservation biology has been a widely debated topic for almost 40 years. It's a challenge to scientifically prove the existence of traps because, by definition, a trap leads to a population decline or even local extinction. Most studies aren't long enough to demonstrate that.

Another fundamental of ecological trap theory is that most often, traps occur in habitats that have been altered by man. There are instances where unaltered habitats have exhibited trap characteristics, but for the most part, traps are found where humans have changed the natural world. And the faster the change occurs, the more likely animals will be duped by the new trap.

Animals are fooled by traps in part because they often have to make habitat decisions long before the trap springs. An alfalfa field cut to within a few inches of the ground wouldn't tempt a hen pheasant. But she makes her nesting decision when the alfalfa is growing lush and tall.

Animals may eventually learn to avoid the traps. However, adaptation takes time. In the example of the pheasant hens, the trap was fatal, making adaptation on their part unlikely. Only hens that survived by flushing early could choose different habitat later if the allure of the trap wasn't too strong.

Although traps may be likened to a sink or drain for a population, true sinks are actually on the opposite end of the scale. A trap attracts animals and may even be superior habitat until the trap is sprung. Sinks, on the other hand, are poor quality habitats avoided until better habitats are full. Or as one biologist put it, "traps are sink habitats that are preferred rather than avoided."

Ecological traps are, in my opinion, worse than sinks. Animals avoid sinks until there is nowhere else to go. In a sense, the population has reached its carrying capacity and can grow no larger until habitat limiting factors are addressed.

Traps, on the other hand, may draw wildlife from other more suitable but less attractive habitats and actually impact populations. There is the double whammy: humans remove habitat from wildlife production then bait the wildlife back in to sure death. Somehow that doesn't seem fair.

Ecological Traps Part 2

Urban areas offer good hunting for a variety of raptors and a number of them, including peregrine falcons and Cooper's hawks, have adapted to city life. However, in Tucson, Arizona, the Cooper's hawks have entered into an ecological trap they cannot see. Researchers compared the nesting success between those inside the city where abundant pigeons and doves make life easy, and those in surrounding natural habitats. Well fed city hawks hatch more young than their rural cousins and if the story stopped there, there would be no trap. But rural hawks fledge four times as many chicks as the city hawks because the prey of the city hawks is infected with a parasite that kills their chicks. The city population steadily drops but the decline is masked by young rural hawks moving to the city, enticed by the illusion of easy living.

Without an understanding of ecological traps, a manager's response to this situation might be to increase protection of Cooper's hawk habitat outside the city. That would just continue to supply hawks to flush down the drain. Instead, the focus should be on reducing the effectiveness or attraction of the trap.

Canals and ditches are another ecological trap and a steady drain on fish populations. Fish are often attracted to canals and ditches just as they would be to any side channel or stream. However, once in the system, they may be trapped by headgates or rapidly changing water levels. Only barriers such as fish screens can alleviate this population drain.

Land managers have to be particularly careful not to create ecological traps in the name of restoration as happened in the Negev Desert of Israel. In an attempt to improve habitat for an endangered lizard, managers planted groves of thorny shrubs in an environment where shrubs had been sparse. Lizards were indeed impressed with their efforts and immediately began to use the new habitat. Eleven years later, almost no lizards could be found. Researchers determined that the shrubs provided new perching habitat for shrikes and kestrels, two of the lizard's top predators. However, since the lizards were not adapted to judge habitat suitability based on vertical structure, they did not perceive the risk and continued to use the trap until they were nearly extirpated. Fortunately, the researchers were able to convince the managers not to plant any more "habitat."

As I drove along I-15 several days ago, I marveled at all the wasted space between the north and south bound lanes. I wondered briefly how we could take advantage of that space for habitat. Then I remembered picking up several road killed barn owls along this stretch and it quickly dawned on me that any habitat "improvement" would create a trap. Animals would indeed appreciate what we could do, but everything attracted there would get flattened by traffic. Clearly, the best management approach would be to make the medians and shoulders as inhospitable as possible and just accept the loss of habitat, which incidentally, equates to about 35 acres per linear mile of interstate.

I see myself in all this. I am routinely lured into what seems like a good deal or easy living, only to discover that something tasty or shiny was actually the bait in a cleverly disquised trap.

Spotting Wildlife

Being able to spot wildlife is an art and a skill. It may even be genetic although not necessarily hereditary. My paternal grandmother routinely shamed the men in her family by spotting wildlife first. It was her gift, but it wasn't passed on to me. I am terminally handicapped when it comes to being the first to spot an animal.

For instance, some people can spot wildlife driving 75 mph down the interstate. Not me. I am focused on the road because of a natural tendency to drive where I look. If I am scanning the fields left and right, that's where I'll end up.

And, hunting seems to compound my challenges in spotting wildlife. I can't count how many rocks, stumps, branches and shadows I have tried to turn into deer or elk. To my credit though, I have never tried to shoot one.

As a poor wildlife spotter, my strategy to deal with the deficient gene was to marry someone truly gifted in that arena. My wife is a great and enthusiastic wildlife spotter. For instance, once I nearly crashed the car when she spotted an owl on a tall post near the high school and screamed excitedly. It was plastic, but she correctly identified it as a great horned owl.

While at a marina in the Everglades, she spotted four owls at once. She breathlessly urged me to grab the camera for the shot of a lifetime. I was in no hurry, though, because they weren't going anywhere. Besides, photos of plastic owls, placed on the pylons to frighten off the gulls, really aren't hot sellers.

The owl incidents made her leery of all wildlife encounters for awhile. Later, still in the Everglades, we came upon a very large and very motionless alligator. It looked dead to me (we had seen several dead ones) but not to be fooled again, she was convinced that someone had placed a wooden one there as a joke. I bounced a few pebbles off its armored hide and its eyes popped open, sending us both back a couple feet in a hurry.

In the Lamar Valley of Yellowstone, she saw what she thought was a large flock of dark colored geese. It broke my heart to have to tell her that they were bedded bison. Same trip, geese at Norris were certainly deer and the tall, stately sandhill cranes could become almost anything. But, at least she is seeing the critters. We can team up on identification.

There are some wildlife imitations that are actually too easy to spot. Black, life-sized silhouettes of wildlife are becoming common yard ornaments. I am sure they are causing their share of auto accidents among others with my particular driving ailment. My neighbor has one and it still occasionally catches me off-guard in the morning to look out across the back lawn and see a bull moose, partly because that is a totally real possibility just about anywhere in the Upper Snake River Valley.

I never took up golf, reasoning that I didn't need one more hobby to execute poorly. But, even if I never develop a wildlife spotting gene, it's one interest I'll never give up.

Facing the Wolves

The cow elk stood alone on a scrap of an island in Nymph Lake in the heart of Yellowstone Park. Three wolves, a black and two grays, lounged confidently on the bank, making her chance of escape look bleak. They knew their prey was cornered and the odds clearly favored them.

The game began at 5:30 in the morning. A tourist videotaped the wolves as they tore at her flanks and chased the elk down the middle of the Grand Loop road two miles north of Norris. Bloodied and desperate, she sought refuge in the water. A tragic mistake, because now she was trapped.

She stood and faced the wolves for nearly 13 hours on that island. She watched each move, anxious but defiant, shifting her weight occasionally to favor her injuries.

As I watched, I wondered what was going through her mind. Was she plotting an escape? Was she measuring her chances of success? If nothing else, surely she felt terribly alone and afraid. No big bull would come to her rescue; hers was a solitary fight and she and the calf she still carried faced almost certain death.

A human dimension to the struggle lined the road. The young ranger chided well over 100 pedestrians to stay behind the cones and cautioned drivers to park completely outside the white line.

The humans were strangely at odds with their feelings. Overwhelmingly, the crowd's sentiments raged for the elk. "I want her to live," stated one woman. "I don't want to see the kill," exclaimed another. Yet they stayed, anticipating, and even hoping for the moment when the wolves would make their final attack.

The daylong stand-off exhausted the cow and around 6:15 p.m., she lay down, and unwittingly energized the wolves. The black wolf circled the lake to come in from behind. In position, he made his move, splashing into the water at a run. The elk was up in an instant and immediately headed for deeper water where the wolf would be forced to swim.

The cow attacked as the wolf closed the gap. Her front feet flailed in a spray of water. Repulsed, the wolf retreated and tried again. The cow fought well, but, when the second wolf joined the fray, she was in trouble. Several times they dragged her down and the fight appeared over. Each time though, she managed to regain her footing and shake off her attackers.

Her luck ran out when the other gray wolf joined in. The grays finally grabbed her on each flank while the black clamped his jaws on her throat. She struggled and fought but the chokehold robbed her of breath and life and she buckled under the onslaught. The wolves claimed their kill and began to tear at her before her last kicks were stilled.

As I walked away, I pondered the lesson of the day. We all face wolves in life and no one wants to be the one pulled down. Like the elk though, we are most vulnerable alone. With no friends to watch our back, no family to step up and help us fight or catch us when we fall, we too can be overwhelmed. I realized that the wolves may howl at us all day long, but they'll stay at bay so long as we stand together.

Anthropomorphism

My latest nature column had barely hit managing editor Rob Thornberry's desk before I had a message to call him. Our visit went something like this:

Me: "Rob, Terry Thomas returning your call."

Rob: "Your column."

Me: "Yes?" (The column Rob was referring to was *Facing the Wolves*, one I thought might earn me a little praise).

Rob: "Anthropomorphizing."

Me: "Yes?"

Rob: "Don't do it. I don't like it. I'll let it slide this time (that's editor speak for, 'dang, it works but it violates convention'). In fact, I would like a column on why people anthropomorphize at all."

End of conversation.

My offense was to write of confident wolves and a lonely, frightened cow elk plotting an escape. Confident, plotting, lonely, and frightened are, in most estimations, emotions reserved only for the human species, hence I was assigning human qualities to an animal: anthropomorphism.

Guilty as charged. In my defense, my misdeed is certainly not as pernicious as Bambi or Sponge Bob, the Lion King, Charlotte and her barnyard gang, or the whole Alice In Wonderland thing which was banned in 1911 in parts of China for giving animals human language and putting humans and animals on the same level. These are truly anthropomorphism extremes: animals having a human experience. They are misleading and create an unrealistic view of nature.

Take Bambi, for instance. In the real world, a deer wouldn't even know his father and would be driven off by his mother at one year of age. He wouldn't judge right from wrong, see things from another's perspective or make decisions based on mercy, honor, love, or integrity. He responds based on how to best fill the three "S's": survival, sustenance, and sex.

When we assign human traits to animals, we often fall into the trap of expecting them to behave that way. The young man killed by wolves in Canada, and the late Timmy Treadwell, self-proclaimed brother of the grizzly, are two examples where anthropomorphism ended in tragedy.

But, on the other hand, is it just human arrogance that assumes that animals are merely driven by stimulus and have no emotion at all? Are emotions the exclusive realm of the human species or are we jealously guarding what we believe makes us a higher form of life?

My dog would nearly wiggle out of her skin when we returned from a long absence. Would it be wrong to describe her state as joyous or happy? Any dog owner would struggle to find any other way to express it. She may or may not have actually *"felt"* that way but she *acted* in a manner consistent with how we would feel in a similar situation. We use our own experience to describe it.

One website dedicated to understanding anthropomorphism stated, "We often attach traits to animals and objects when their behavior matches our stereotypes of these traits in people. Doing so is probably automatic. It helps us to predict behavior and form expectations".

There you have it: we anthropomorphize because it is in our nature to do so. Journalistically, anthropomorphism is like spice and should be used sparingly. And, it probably doesn't belong in a serious, no nonsense, just the facts, kind of nature column. But then, who wants to read (or write) one of those?

The Trouble with Being Male

In my house, I am respected, not for my brains, but for my brawn. This is especially true during yard work season. Spading, rototilling, and moving very big and heavy things seems to be what I am good for.

Surely, males of other species have it better than I do. What about ducks? The males of many species mate with as many females as they can and then abandon the hens and the family. Like teenage boys, the drakes hang together to fight and brag about their conquests and eat junk food.

There is a downside for male ducks, though. Most often, drake plumage is bright and colorful, necessary to interest as many hens as possible. The females are drably decked out in camouflage. That makes males easier targets for predators and sought by hunters.

Promiscuity among males brings its own set of challenges even beyond the world of ducks. If a male can breed with 5-10 females, fewer males are needed. Any time males can be readily distinguished from the females—ducks, elk, and pheasant come to mind—the males can be hunted like a separate species with male- only seasons. I'll take yard work.

In the world of spiders, males definitely have it worse than I do. Often, the female is larger and likely to consume the male after mating. Males have to be truly dedicated to the concept of perpetuating the species to accept those terms.

What about a buck deer? Surely his is a life of pleasure and leisure. Except during the summer, of course, when he heads to the high, gnarly country, leaving the sweet, productive habitat to the ladies and their fawns. And when the rut comes, he may spend several weeks hardly eating at all as he gathers, breeds, and defends his harem.

And, then, there are those antlers. He has to grow them from scratch each season, using nutrients that could be laying on fat for the winter. Until they harden and die, antlers are tender living tissue and bumping one is painful. Worse, with antlers, size truly is everything. If his aren't big enough, the does will ignore his advances.

Males of many species must compete or fight for the right to breed. This is natural selection at its finest, ensuring that the strongest genes get passed on. It's a great system if you are the big stud on the block. Everyone else plays second fiddle.

It is not uncommon for fighting for the right to breed to end in injury or death of one or both of the combatants. But, a testosterone overload smothers reason like a blanket, making death seem like a small price to pay to be king of the mountain for a day.

Maybe the alpha wolf has it best. He is king of his pack, is the only male to mate, and the pack helps to raise his family. Sweet. But, he also has to defend the pack against other packs, and with bared fangs, constantly answers challenges to his supremacy. It is almost a given that he will die in battle or from his wounds after having lost everything he fought so hard to win.

I suppose I will just keep the life I have. In comparison to male life in the wild, being the brawn in my family isn't all that bad.

The Aster Family

Natural selection has been more kind to some families of species than to others. Families that have had the misfortune of evolving to fit a very specific set of circumstances, such as a particular island chain, are highly vulnerable to extinction. But a family of species that is widely adapted to broad and varying ecological conditions can thrive when others fade.

The Asteraceae family of plants is one such widely adapted family. With almost 25,000 species, it is one of the largest plant families on this planet. Members are distributed around the globe and almost from pole to pole. There are numerous herbaceous members but also lots of shrub species, some vines and even a few epiphytes, aquatic species, and trees in the family.

Everyone is familiar with members of this family, although at a glance, you might never guess that so many wildly different species can be related. Chefs appreciate this family for lettuce, artichokes, sunflowers, tarragon, and safflowers. Herbal tea enthusiasts hold it in high regard because it is the family that produces chamomile, echinacea, and calendula. Gardeners are dazzled by daisies, gayflowers, cosmos, dahlias, marigolds, zinnias, and chrysanthemums.

Outside the garden, this family includes species important to wildlife and insects including: sagebrush, rabbitbrush, yarrow, balsamroot, dandelions, prickly lettuce, fleabanes, arnicas, and senecios. And the family bad boys include; knapweeds, yellow star thistle, hawkweeds, and Canada, musk, bull, and plumeless thistles.

As can be expected in such a large family, it is impossible to find many characteristics shared by all. For instance, leaf patterns may be whorled, opposite, or alternate with edges that are smooth to toothed, entire (unlobed) to deeply lobed, with or without prickles. They thrive in just about every type of habitat from high alpine to desert to tropical forest.

The one unifying characteristic in this huge family is the inflorescence or flower structure. At one time, this family was named Compositae, because, although the flower structure may look like a single flower, it is really a grouping of a few to many individual flowers that together have the appearance of a single flower.

Think about a sunflower head. A single head is comprised of hundreds of individual sessile (stemless) flowers that share a single receptacle. This type of flower structure is called a capitulum. The individual flowers usually have no visible sepals but bracts that look and function like sepals often surround the capitulum.

The flowers around the edge of the capitulum have a ligule, which is a single broad strap of petal, and are called ray flowers. If these flowers are divided lengthwise down the strap, they are bilaterally symmetrical, but the inner side is very different from the ligule side. Regardless, each petal or ligule represents a separate flower and each produces a seed.

Within the center of a sunflower, there are disk flowers. These have no strap but are bilaterally symmetrical no matter how they are divided. Each produces one seed.

The sunflower isn't the model for all species in this diverse family. Some have only ray flowers, others only disk flowers and the exact design is variable. Nonetheless, all this variability has built an astounding amount of resiliency in this family. It will probably be around long after the human family self-destructs.

Water: A Wildlife Magnet

I was working on a hunch. Even though the maps didn't show it, somewhere in this large, isolated finger of timber there had to be water. I knew that I wasn't looking for a stream; that would have been obvious. It must be a seep or a spring, something a map might miss.

It took less than an hour to find it and it was more than I had hoped. Twenty yards wide, the muddy ring around the outside was full of elk tracks and one set of black bear tracks. Incredibly, it was also apparent that no livestock had used the water hole in a very long time, if ever, and it was devoid of human sign as well. I had found Nirvana.

I set up my blind and camera and settled in to wait to see what would show up. I didn't wait long. Three modest-sized bull elk emerged from the timber on the opposite side of the pond and strode confidently to the water's edge. They drank and then frolicked in the water like calves. Another bull came from behind me, barking his displeasure at finding me set up literally in his trail.

When I reluctantly gathered my blind after less than three hours at the water hole, I had seen six bull elk, a pine marten, a great gray owl, gray jays, red-breasted nuthatches, dark-eyed juncos and several other birds I couldn't identify.

My experience points out that the equation for seeing wildlife is simple: water = wildlife. Whether they live in it, on it, around it or just drink it, the vast majority of species need water daily. So, you can't go wrong looking for wildlife around water.

Riparian areas, those green narrow strips of shrubs and trees along streams and rivers, are great places to look for wildlife. They have the most diverse array of wildlife species of any habitat type. One study conducted by the Forest Service in Oregon found that 359 of 414 animal species studied used riparian or wetland habitats for all or part of their lives. The Environmental Protection Agency indicates that more birds use riparian areas than all other western habitats combined. Multistoried riparian zones such as those along the Snake River have the highest biodiversity, but find any healthy riparian zone winding through otherwise arid county and you will be surprised at all the wildlife you can see.

When marshes, bogs and other types of wetlands are included, up to 75 percent of Idaho's wildlife depend upon water for a least one portion of their life cycle. Since wetlands and riparian areas make up only one percent of the land area, the search zone for most wildlife is actually very small.

For observing wildlife, though, nothing beats a watering hole, spring, or seep to concentrate critters. When water is scarce, these are the places all wildlife have to visit to satisfy their need for hydration. All that is required is a blind to conceal your outline and movement, and patience. The more time spent patiently waiting, the more species you are likely to see.

Oh, and bring your own water. You likely won't want to be sharing what the wildlife drink.

Bearpaw Fire

One October day, my wife and I found ourselves in Grand Teton National Park. It was a beautiful, clear, and calm morning to watch elk, but as afternoon approached, a huge pillar of smoke began to rise from the south end of Jackson Lake. The Bearpaw Fire, started by lightning on August 30th, was being agitated by afternoon winds.

A few days before, this fire had been a smoldering sleeper on a peninsula between Spaulding Bay and Leigh Lake. It was monitored by a National Park Service fire management team, but initially provided little in the way of excitement.

A stiff north wind on September 25th changed that. From ten acres to 1,000 acres in 24 hours, the fire threatened to race around the south end of the lake. The fire management team fought the fire on the southeast side to make sure the fire did not reach Signal Mountain Lodge, but the rest of the fire was allowed to burn for resource benefit.

Three weeks later, I returned and wandered through some of the burn. Still not declared officially out, I found areas where the fire still punked through a foot-thick duff of pine needles, exposing mineral soil.

The fire perimeter encompassed a total of 2,844 acres but, like most fires, not everything within the perimeter was black. The fire created an awesome mosaic of burned, partly burned, and unburned areas. This type of habitat diversity maximizes wildlife habitat.

For all who grew up under Smokey Bear's influence, this concept of fire actually being good for a forest may still be hard to understand. Many systems, though, evolved with fire and need it to maintain their functions.

Frequent fire can actually protect forests from more severe fire events. Fire at routine intervals removes excess fuels, thins the forests and creates natural fire breaks. If the entire forest were managed this way, "catastrophic" fires would be rare indeed.

Jackie Skaggs, Public Information Officer for the park, reminded me, "Fire resets the biological clock and allows colonizing species a chance to thrive." Indeed, a dark shady forest is really poor habitat for many species of plants and animals. It is estimated that less than one third of the wildlife species exist in a mature conifer forest when compared to an earlier seral stage such as aspen.

It is the same with vegetation. With this fire, we could expect to see grasses, forbs, shrubs and aspens flourish in the burned areas now that sunlight can again reach the forest floor. Species that have been all but absent under the conifers will thrive and the amount of forage produced will skyrocket. For the next several years wildflowers in the burn area should be fantastic.

The fire certainly reduced habitat for some deep-forest wildlife species but improved habitat for others. Woodpeckers will move in quickly to search for insects in the dead trees. Cavity nesting birds will follow the woodpeckers. Deer, elk, moose, and bears will all benefit from the improved forage.

This autumn the forests have been alive with color. If we want them to stay that way, we would do well to remember that in this context, black is a color too.

Food Caching

I jealously guard my desk at work. It isn't because I am hiding contraband or am just territorial; rather, my desk is a food cache. On any given day, there might be pretzels, a candy bar or two, protein bars, jerky, and cans of soup and tuna. My cache is a hedge against the ravages of winter.

But I am not the only winter hoarder. Sure, bears, bats, and ground squirrels have given winter the cold shoulder, choosing to sleep their way to spring. And migrants have long since abandoned us for sunnier climes. But, like me, many mammals and birds that stay behind to bravely face winter also cache summer groceries when food is abundant and depend on it during the winter months.

There are two basic food caching strategies. The first is to put it all in just a few caches, called hoards, and then staunchly defend them. A good example of this approach is the honeybee hive. Bees don't have to spend energy trying to remember where the winter grocery store is and they are equipped to defend their supply as it builds. Of course, should they lose the hoard, the result could be catastrophic for the hive.

The other general strategy is called scatter caching. This stratagem reasons that with enough small caches, there will still be plenty left even if a few are plundered.

Most birds and mammals that cache food use this tactic. However, it does exact a higher energy cost because they must remember where the food is stored.

The simplest form of finding food caches is called re-foraging and is especially effective if the food source has a detectable scent. Many species of rodents practice this type of caching because it doesn't require extensive memory. In short, they gather food sources from afar and cache them in easy-to-find locations inside their home range. When they are hungry, they search likely spots within a much smaller area. The caches are easy to recover, but energy isn't wasted on memory.

Another tactic is called foraging by rule: the animal hides the food in specific types of habitat—for example, only under rocks on a south-facing slope. When it is hungry, it only searches those specific locations, again saving the energy drain an increased memory requires.

But the most advanced food stashers scatter cache, often over broad areas, and can remember precisely where each cache is using a series of landmarks. These animals have a well developed hippocampus; the center of the brain responsible for short and long term memory and spatial navigation. Chickadees, squirrels, foxes, and more are scatter cachers. But members of the corvid family, including ravens, jays, and nutcrackers, are exceptional at this. A chickadee starts to lose memory of cache locations after about 28 days, but some corvids can remember the location of caches after 250 days.

Some birds may have hundreds or even thousands of caches, but even then, recovery of the booty isn't haphazard. In a study of black capped chickadees, researchers found that the birds remembered which caches had the preferred foods and recovered them first.

I realized that my strategy is scatter caching by rule. I often forget exactly where I put something, but I know the likely places to look. Sometimes my caches are empty and that's a disappointment. Yet, sometimes I find a forgotten cache and it is like an extra pay day—or is that PayDay?

Plundering the Cache

Now that the word is out that I have a food cache in my desk, I trust no one; and even cleverly concealed food is at risk without lock and key. The only other thing that protects my stash is that I tend to cache food only a truly desperate scoundrel would even consider edible.

In the wild, food caches are never without risk either. Discovery of almost any cache is like walking into a free grocery store for most species. Bears, in particular, seem to make cache plundering a sport. With their keen sense of smell, little escapes notice and few caches can be so securely guarded or protected that a bear can't ravage them.

Food caching is generally a solitary and selfish event, even among species that live communally. Food is cached and retrieved in secret and consumed alone; and family and friends are not to be trusted because everyone pilfers, leaving no cache safe.

In a perfect bird world, caching and pilfering from friends, family, and conspecifics (strangers of the same species) would balance each other out. Theoretically, birds cache and steal from each other in relatively similar proportions with no net gain or loss; thus pilfering shouldn't raise any hackles. It is really more like reciprocal cache sharing. Apparently, birds don't see it that way, though.

A study involving ravens bore this out. Researchers tested both wild and captive ravens to see how they behaved when it came to caching food. Food-caching birds were very cautious not to be seen when they hoarded food. They slinked away from other ravens and usually placed a visual obstacle between them and potential thieves before hiding their food.

On the other hand, birds hoping to steal food from caches actually acted nonchalant, and tried to appear not to take notice of the cachers. If the caching bird wasn't paying attention, the marauder got a free lunch. But if the caching bird saw them coming, even the indifference ploy triggered a reaction: the cachers frequently interrupted caching, changed cache sites, or recovered their food items.

Caching and pilphering are mutually serious businesses and both the thieves and the cachers are energetic in their respective roles, even though the roles routinely reverse. From the bird perspective, caching and stealing could be summed up in one word: More. A perfect day might be to raid a number of caches, re-cache the plunder and not have a single new cache discovered by conspecifics or family.

But, not all species are selfish. There are a few species that actually share food caches. The beaver is one. Food, in the form of green twigs and sticks, is stored under water behind their ponds. When food is recovered and brought to the lodge to eat, all members of the family partake equally.

Acorn woodpeckers are another example of true shared food hoarding. Members of the community all bring food supplies to a communal larder. All community members feed from the same stores.

Through all this intrigue, there is an ecological value of caching. Most years, not all caches are recovered. The animal either forgets about the cache, dies before it can recover all the food, or stores more than it can use. Thus, caching becomes an integral part of seed dispersal, with many of the seeds literally planted by the cachers. I suppose that explains why I have a pretzel sapling growing out of my pencil drawer.

Burrs Under Your Saddle

A friend of mine is an aficionado of Great Pyrenees dogs—the huge sheep guard dogs with long white fur. One fall day, his dog came back from a romp in the field and flopped down on the carpet. A few minutes later, the dog tried to rise but was stuck to the rug. His long hair, loaded with burdock burs, had him fastened to the shag!

If you have been wandering about lately, you probably can relate to this poor dog. Burrs are an aggravating element of the fall woods, getting tangled in socks, shirts, and even hair.

As irritating as burrs are, they are really quite an ingenious way to distribute seeds. Burrs are seedpods and their purpose is to insure that seed from the mother plant is disbursed to as many locales as possible. When a burr attaches itself to an animal's fur, there is no telling where it, and the seeds it carries, will end up.

Most burrs use some form of barb to attach themselves to passersby. In fact, burrs similar to those found on burdock were the inspiration for the now famous hook-and-loop closure system we often refer to as Velcro©. Indeed, when I look closely at the business end of a burdock burr, it looks exactly like the hook portion of Velcro©.

Burdock plants can be over six feet tall. They have huge leaves and clusters of round burrs at the ends of the branches. The unforgiving burrs are so "sticky" that they can become a death trap for small animals such as hummingbirds and bats.

I have often observed moose and elk in the winter that were literally covered in burdock burrs. The burrs work themselves into the hair so tightly that they are only released when the animal finally sheds its winter coat.

Houndstongue is another burr we love to hate. It forms that irritating little pancake shaped burr that seems to wrap itself into the threads of your socks. If you happen to cruise through a patch with a wool sweater, you could find yourself throwing the sweater away.

Nothing can make a bigger knot out of shoe laces than the stick-tight burrs. These are tiny randomly shaped burrs with 5-9 spines, each with minute hooks that can make a terrible mess of just about any fabric. At least burdock burrs are big enough to get a grip on. The small stick-tight burrs are sometimes impossible to remove.

Wild licorice, a native burr, seems to be rapidly spreading. I am seeing it in more places all the time, attesting to the efficiency of burrs as a seed dispersal tactic. Wild licorice is a medium sized annual plant with compound leaves like a honey locust. The burr is oblong and bright brown colored. I actually considered it quite handsome until I began hunting pheasant near Beaver Dick Park in Madison County. A few hours of hunting was matched by an equal number of hours painstakingly removing the licorice burrs from the long hair of my golden retriever. Many were so tightly entwined that scissors were my only option.

As irritating as they are, a few burrs shouldn't keep you in the house. But, unless you want more burrs next year, don't pull the burrs from your clothes and toss these seed capsules on the ground. Carefully remove them and place them in a bag and put them in the trash or the fire.

Animal Communication

A low, powerful bellow rolled across the tranquil Everglades air. The call was repeated by a dozen alligators up and down the marsh until the air vibrated from the sound. We could literally feel it as well as hear it. Bull alligators were declaring their territory. We stood on the boardwalk several feet above the numerous alligators along this trail, listening to the roars surrounding us, feeling vulnerable in the midst of so many predators.

I don't know why, but it came as a surprise that alligators vocalize and have at least six different calls. Vocalization within species is the norm, not the exception, and scientists have spent decades unraveling the different languages of hundreds of species, including alligators.

The study of bio-acoustics, sounds made by animals, has revealed that communication, and vocalizations in particular, play a significant role in animal sociobiology. The attraction of a mate is perhaps the most well-known function of vocalization, but other needs are served as well.

For instance, anyone who has listened carefully to an undisturbed herd of elk realizes that elk routinely talk amongst themselves. The communication helps them to maintain their group unity, recognize individuals, and warn of danger.

While we may enjoy the songs of the robin or the cardinal, they are not singing for our pleasure. Many birds have developed extensive songs to attract a mate and proclaim their territory. Songs are a specific series of notes arranged in a precise pattern. Many birds also have a number of calls used during migration, foraging, and other daily activities. Some birds hatch knowing the songs and calls of their species. Others must learn them from adult birds.

Marine mammals seem to have quite a vocabulary. They recite a large number of chirps, squeaks, hums, and squeals to communicate with each other and to echo-locate. Male humpback whales can be recognized by their long and complex individual songs full of sirens, groans, hums, clicks, and squeals. Each year they sing a new, improved song. Females are impressed by the males with the most multifaceted songs.

Most primates spend their lives in tight-knit groups and have to communicate frequently. They not only have a modest vocabulary but also use smells, facial expressions, ground slapping, and hand gestures to communicate to others in their troop. In captivity, chimpanzees and gorillas have readily learned American Sign Language and have been able to form and interpret actual sentences, likely because sign language is not far removed from their native system of communication.

Sometimes communication is non-vocal but utilizes acoustics just the same. Many insects create specific sounds intended to communicate with others of their species. Grasshoppers and crickets are common examples, producing signals by rubbing hind legs over their forewings. Other insects, such as cicadas, use drum-like membranes to make sounds that can be heard by humans for up to half a mile and may be loud enough to keep you up at night. Still others make sounds far beyond the range of the human ear.

As important as communication is within the animal world, it isn't surprising that human-caused noise pollution is having an impact. In some noisy places, birds cannot hear their own songs or those of rivals. Over several generations, their songs change and are now unrecognizable to their own species, resulting in reduced reproduction. And, low frequency sonar testing by the US military has driven several species of whales out of otherwise suitable habitat.

Whether it is alligators, crickets, chimpanzees, whales, or robins, make no mistake—animals need to communicate with each other just as much as humans do. Communication plays an essential role in the sociobiology of the animal kingdom.

The Eyes Have It

My wife and I occasionally engage in a somewhat morbid discussion: if we had to give up either sight or hearing, which sense could we better live without? Without a doubt Cathy would prefer to lose her eyesight rather than her hearing. I am just the opposite. My eyes are my link to the world, and my connection to the world and life would be severed without them. A few days spent leaf peeping in Tennessee last week re-enforced that—hearing the sounds of autumn was important, but seeing this beautiful corner of the world was essential for complete enjoyment.

Vision is an incredible asset shared by most of the animal kingdom. But it isn't shared equally. In fact, compared to many animals, humans got a raw deal as we have relatively poor eyesight.

Eagles and other raptors are often regarded as having the best eyesight. They can see a prey animal the size of a rabbit from several miles. In contrast, a friend recently put up a long range target at around 1200 yards. It was a white 4 foot square piece of wood with a black center. I barely saw it without binoculars.

But even "best" is a relative term and is based on context. For instance, eagles cannot see at night nearly as well as cats. A cat's night vision comes from elliptical pupils that let in far more light under dim conditions.

Cats and other night hunters, such as owls, also have an extra retinal layer called the tapetum lucidum, which acts like a mirror to reflect and concentrate available light and allows them to see in near total darkness.

Another aspect of visual acuity is the number of vision receptors, called rods and cones, on the retina; the more receptors, the better the vision. Humans have a paltry 200,000 receptors per square millimeter, sending thousands of pulses up the optic nerve every millisecond. A vulture has 1,000,000 per square millimeter but the giant squid, an invertebrate that lives deep in the dark ocean, has up to 1,000,000,000 photoreceptors per square millimeter and commensurately more signals every millisecond.

Eye size is another indicator of sharp vision. The tarsier, a squirrel-sized primate of Southeast Asia, has the largest eyes, proportionately, of any mammal. Each weighs more than its brain. Comparable-sized eyes for a human would be the size of grapefruits. It has extremely acute vision, especially at night.

And with eyes the size of dinner plates, the colossal squid has incredible eyesight even in the near dark of the ocean depths.

Humans can only detect light in what is referred to as the visible spectrum. We are blind to the ultraviolet and infrared range. However, many vertebrate and invertebrate species are able to see these wavelengths. So, the drab-colored bird or insect we see might be incredibly vibrant to its own species.

Insects may have compound eyes, with up to 30,000 individual units called ommatidia, each with a lens and photocells. Each one sees a small portion of the scene, so they might not see things as we do. However, this system allows them to detect even the slightest motion.

There are also physical adaptations that improve visibility. Chameleons not only have incredibly sharp eyesight, but can move their eyes individually, scanning for predators and prey at the same time. The eyes of the four-eyed fish are divided in half, allowing them to see above and below the water simultaneously. The eyes of many prey species are situated on the sides of their heads, giving them up to 270 degrees of vision around them. Human eyes are boring by comparison.

Pitiful as we are, humans do have one unique adaptation: inner vision. No other species can see and create a future. It is a gift we should use wisely.

China's War on Sparrows

In early 1958, China's Chairman, Mao Zedong, faced a dilemma. He had the responsibility to feed half a billion people and he wasn't getting the job done. Of course, none of his advisors would tell him that the system might need a tune-up. One didn't criticize the Chinese Communist government without serious repercussions.

What the advisors needed was something to blame the hunger on, something that could unite the people politically, and also produce more food. After a search that was motivated by a strong desire to not end up on the wrong side of a firing squad, they found their villain.

They solemnly announced to Chairman Mao that diminutive sparrows were responsible for the woes of the massive Chinese agricultural system. They carefully demonstrated to Mao that each sparrow was responsible for consuming up to four pounds of grain per bird per year. With millions of sparrows flitting wantonly about the countryside like flying thieves, the math was simple: the sparrows were getting millions of tons of grain needed to feed the people and that couldn't stand.

Armed with this evidence, Mao declared war on the sparrows based on a simple logic: eliminate the sparrows and improving grain production through better farming practices and conservation of resources would be unnecessary. Stop the sparrow plundering, and storehouses would practically fill themselves.

In Mao's new world, the only good sparrow would be a dead sparrow. At first it must have seemed a daunting task to eliminate all the sparrows from a nation the size of China. But with characteristic socialist zeal, peasants and city dwellers alike united to exterminate what their leaders had identified as a scourge upon land and larder.

And so the war began. Sparrows were shot, bludgeoned, and trapped. Nests were destroyed, chicks killed, and eggs smashed. And, they found, it sometimes wasn't even necessary to physically bash every single sparrow with club or rock. In fact, they didn't need to hit them at all. All they needed to do, they discovered, was to keep the sparrows in frenetic terrified flight without a chance to rest, and their tiny hearts would fail. Organized groups roamed street and field, banging on pots and plates, literally frightening the sparrows to death when they could not land to rest.

The scheme worked. Millions of sparrows—and sparrow meant any small grain eating bird—died. Photographs of roof-high piles of sparrows were sent to Beijing by the hundreds, proof that the people were united and fighting this common enemy.

The next year, Mao was a hero as crop production soared. Storehouses did fill and the peoples' hunger was satiated. But shortsighted plans tend to boomerang and this one did, too. In the fervor to find a scoundrel to blame for poor crops, the role of the sparrows in controlling even greater crop pests was ignored. Without predators, locusts swarmed over the country consuming everything in sight. Mao tried to reverse the disaster; he even imported sparrows from the Soviet Union, but it was too late. Over the next several years, crops were destroyed by insects. As many as 20 million Chinese may have died as an indirect consequence of killing a simple creature like a sparrow.

The ecological chain of interconnectivity had been broken and even with all his political power, Chairman Mao could not escape the consequences. That lesson is still true today.

Hoar Frost

If I have ever been in a truly enchanted kingdom, it was on one incredibly clear and cold morning several years ago. My wife and I topped out on a ridge hoping to find an elk but were instead awed by the sight that greeted us. Everything on top of the ridge—every branch, every blade of grass, every rock—was sheathed with a shimmering white coating of frost that gathered and reflected the morning sun like jeweled prisms.

Mesmerized, I dropped down on my knees for closer examination. The frost was in large, feather-like crystals the size of quarters that glittered in the golden rays of the rising sun. When I barely touched a branch with my mitten, the delicate crystals showered down with the sound of tinkling bells. Fascinated, I nudged another, then another. Until the rising sun ruined my fun, I forgot elk hunting and wandered around touching branches and kicking bushes; watching, listening to, and bathing in the subsequent showers of splendid icy crystals.

What caused this magical condition—one so incredible that even Hollywood's computer simulations couldn't top it? Would I ever see it again or was it a once in a lifetime phenomenon?

The magic that we experienced was exceptional in my experience, but I was pleased to learn that hoar frost, the cause of the phenomenon, is common when conditions are right.

Surface hoar frost is the cold weather equivalent of dew. It forms when water vapor (usually when relative humidity is 70% or more) sublimates onto the surface of objects during very cold and calm weather. During these conditions the earth is losing heat to the atmosphere.

Hoar builds up layer by layer overnight into thin angular crystals. The ones on my magical morning were exceptionally large and appeared as thin as a sheet of paper. There were so many layers that it must have been a very busy night.

Hoar frost can occur anywhere the air is supersaturated with water vapor and temperatures are very cold. Caves and crevasses commonly exhibit hoar frost (creatively called cave frost or crevasse frost). Hoar frost around the entrances to animal burrows (created from saturated exhaled air) is an indicator that the burrows are winter active. Hoar frost build-up between the sticks on a beaver lodge would verify that the lodge is occupied.

Hoar frost can also form deep within a snowpack. This form is called depth hoar. It forms when there is movement of vapor within the snowpack as a result of a temperature gradient. When this happens quickly, it forms unstable layers in the snow because the frost has no binding strength. When these weak layers collapse under the weight of the snow on top, a deadly slab avalanche may occur. These layers are easy to recognize if you dig a snowpit as they collapse readily when disturbed.

Ever since I experienced that enchanted world, I have hoped for a repeat when I was armed with a camera and not a rifle. So far, my luck has not held, but it gives me an excuse to keep looking.

Resources:

Two good books: *Life in the Cold, An introduction to Winter Ecology*. Peter J. Marchand.

The Avalanche Handbook. David McClung and Peter Schaerer.

Natural Sounds

"Go placidly amid the noise and the haste and remember what peace there may be in silence," *Max Ehrmann, 1927.* Is it really silence that brings peace, or rather an absence of human hullabaloo? The wilds that I know are seldom silent, yet peace abounds.

It is impossible in most cases to completely abandon all human distraction when seeking peace in the wilds. A normal human voice, in an otherwise serene setting, can grate like sand in my oatmeal. When my sons and I hunt deer or elk, whispers are the order of the day, as much to preserve the tranquility as to keep from disturbing a buck or bull.

Airplanes are the most pervasive offenders—they are neither predictable nor avoidable as their noise pollution builds, peaks and then declines. Yet even here, I am conflicted. Once, when two roaring Air Force fighter jets skimmed over the high mountain pass in which I was standing, I found the thunderous technological marvels exhilarating. But that was an exception—airplane noise is usually an affront to solitude and serenity.

In autumn, no sound in the woods stirs my soul like the bugle of a bull elk. It is a dichotomous love too, for I relish the far off whistle as it echoes down a canyon every bit as much as the unmistakable, deep, reverberating, and penetrating bugle, felt as much as heard, as a bull strides in close.

Whether it is waves rhythmically gliding up a beach or rain cascading on a tent, nothing soothes quite like the sound of water in motion. I am drawn to tumbling brooks like a returning salmon to its home stream. Tension fades as I lie back and listen to the timeless and endless chorus as the water falls, skitters, and twists through granite slabs or boulders or slips more quietly down a moss covered course.

If there is a natural sound that really vexes my soul, it is the rattling of dried mules' ears leaves against my boots when I strive for stealth on the hunt. The later crunch of fallen leaves, though, is a welcome sound, a paradox that leads me to believe that context and timing, and not the sound, are the issue.

Other sounds fill the woods, as well, when you really stop to listen. Birds call, woodpeckers tap, jays mimic the sounds they hear, a raven's wings "wump" as it flies overhead. The cry of a red-tailed hawk carries well as it rides the thermals. The belligerent red squirrel chatters angrily at any and all intrusions into his territory, and the autumn woods are often filled with the sound of squirrels' collective harvest of pine cones hitting the ground like leaden rain. All of these sounds are as they should be. The woods may be peaceful but are rarely silent.

Wind is the most ubiquitous of wild sounds. Often it is the background symphony for all the stellar solo performances. But wind creates its own sound too. Trees creak and sway under its intoxicating influence, and mute reminders of this invisible force litter the forest floor. Whether it is a kissing whisper or a roar from high places like Windy Devil Saddle, wind is a subject all its own.

A calm starry night is the closest thing to true silence in the woods. As the hubbub of the day subsides, day sounds are traded for the hum of the night. Owls hoot, crickets stride, frogs call. On the rare, truly still night, the snap of a distant twig under the foot of an unseen creature can sound like a gunshot and fire the primal imagination.

Step into the woods, walk along the river, or climb a mountain peak and experience the tranquility and grace only the outdoors can offer. Just don't expect it to be quiet.

How Do They Do That?

Even though I have trained and worked in the wildlife field for many years, I am still astounded by what I see and what I read about. How do animals do some of the things they do? For some questions, there are scientific answers, while others are really still a mystery. Even so, science may understand the "Why" but the "How" and "How-It-Came-To-Be" departments or vice versa, are still often lacking. Regardless of the fact that we may understand the process on some scientific level, the things animals do are just amazing.

Here is my short list of fascinating animal accomplishments:

- How do birds in a flock all turn at the same time? From a casual observer's perspective, it appears that the flock is one giant organism weaving and dodging like wisps of magical smoke.
- How do schools of fish do the same thing?
- How do homing pigeons find their way home, often over incredible distances? I can't tell north from south without the sun or a compass and have been lost more times than I can count, so how does something with a brain smaller than a pea…uh, let's not go there.
- To prove that point, I spent much of Veteran's Day confused on a mountain I know well. How then, does the Arctic Tern find its way from the tip of North America to Antarctica and back again (10,000 miles one way!), especially the first time, when it has never been there?
- How do salmon unerringly detect the waters from their home stream diluted in a river to a concentration measuring in the billionths and follow it back to their natal ground?
- How did pika figure out that dry vegetation stores well but uncured vegetation does not?
- How do ants carry such incredible loads, up to 50 times their body weight, when carrying half my weight would put me in a body cast?
- How can skunks stand each other? Is it a smell only another skunk can love?

- How do bears go all winter without taking a pee, when I can't go all night?
- Animal communication is always fascinating, but how did honeybees develop a system of communication, a dance of sorts, to tell other bees the location of a good source of nectar? The dance tells other bees the direction, distance, and quality of the new find. This system is so advanced that bioengineers are studying it for applications in the field of resource allocation.
- How do cats (not really wildlife) always land right side up? I tested this extensively as a kid and found that it worked every time despite energetic scientific attempts to prove the opposite.
- How do bighorn sheep rams butt heads with such terrific force and not break their necks? It apparently doesn't even give them a headache because they keep doing it!
- Why do we have house cats, anyway?
- And of course, the epitome of amazement, how do porcupines make love?

This is just a very small list of the remarkable things animals do. I continually research topics such as these, but only occasionally find answers (at least that I can understand).

Even if science can unravel the magic, it doesn't tarnish the fact that creatures we consider mere animals have resolved some pretty complex challenges. Just imagine what they could do with opposable thumbs.

In Memoriam

We spent Memorial Day recreating in less than ideal weather and we saw much of it from inside the car. It did afford us time to reminisce though, about our servicemen and about a growing list of people in our lives—grandparents, Cathy's brother, my mother, a niece, and most recently, a cousin, who had passed on. These people blessed our days—we are thankful for them and miss them.

The Earth, too, has suffered kindred losses. Dinosaurs, mastodons, Irish elk—all now extinct species. Five extinction periods have occurred in the past, each tied to a cataclysmic natural disaster such as a meteor collision with the earth or a super volcano.

Extinction isn't always natural. According to the US Fish and Wildlife Service, over 500 North American species, subspecies, and varieties of animals and plants have become extinct since the Pilgrims landed at Plymouth. Some took centuries to fade out, but others, such as Stellar's sea cow, a gentle three ton beast of the Aleutian Islands of Alaska, was hunted to extinction in 30 years. Carolina parakeets, dodo birds, and many more suffered similar unnatural extinctions.

Most scientists agree that today, the rate of extinction far exceeds the natural expected rate. They estimate that within 100 years, 50% of the world's current species of flora and fauna will be extinct.

Unlike all other extinctions, this sixth extinction is being caused by one species, Man. One scientist has termed humans, "the exterminator species." In the name of progress, we eradicate species haphazardly, not considering their place or value in the world. Aldo Leopold warned, "To keep every cog and wheel is the first precaution of intelligent tinkering," yet we are casting off parts and pieces with abandon.

The passenger pigeon is an oft cited example of a man-caused extinction. At one time numbering in the billions, by 1920 they were extinct. That is old news. What is telling though, is the attitude of the 1857 Ohio Senate when they declined to pass a bill to protect the passenger pigeon: "The passenger pigeon needs no protection. Wonderfully prolific, having the vast forests of the North as its breeding grounds, traveling hundreds of miles in search of food, it is here today and elsewhere tomorrow, and no ordinary destruction can lessen them, or be missed from the myriads that are yearly produced."

Pigeon numbers had apparently dwindled enough to cause alarm, but not enough to convince legislators to meddle with the healthy commerce surrounding the bird—pigeons by the train car load were being shipped to eastern markets. I doubt that even a look into a crystal ball would have swayed the Ohio Senate.

On May 14, 2008, the polar bear was listed as threatened under the Endangered Species Act. I know, it seems preposterous, impossible, than an icon like the polar bear could be threatened with extinction, or that we are playing a part in it. We could be like the 1857 Ohio Senate and publicly declare it to be impossible and continue on like nothing is wrong. Or, we can accept responsibility and generate changes now, while there is still time.

But, this really isn't just about polar bears. It's about an idea—whether it is a polar bear or an ant, each and every species has an intrinsic value and we need them more than they need us. If the Earth mourns the loss of half its species in the next hundred years, Man will be the biggest loser.

Carrying Capacity

Ask any biologist what "carrying capacity" or "K" is and you are likely to get a theoretical textbook answer something like this: Carrying capacity is the maximum number of a certain species that can be supported indefinitely by their habitat without damaging said habitat. That makes a lot of sense, theoretically.

But theory goes out the window when someone actually tries to apply that textbook definition to a given wildlife population. Theoretical carrying capacity searches for a static number in a world defined by annual and long-term changes to the habitat.

In the real world, resources don't remain constant, so "K" is always in flux. Carrying capacity is manipulated by so many influences that it is often impossible to produce much more than a rough estimate. Competing uses that diminish resources (competition from both man and beast), drought, hard winters, fire and more, all impact carrying capacity, yet are usually unpredictable and unmeasureable in their effect.

Carrying capacity can change rapidly at times. Fires during the early 1900s in the Clearwater area of North-Central Idaho burned hundreds of thousands of acres of mature forest, a great loss of elk habitat, or so it seemed. It wasn't long though, before shrubs and grasses recovered and elk populations exploded as the carrying capacity of their habitat increased.

Because of the improved habitat, for many years the Lochsa and Selway Rivers had the reputation of some of the best hunting in the West. Gradually though, habitat quality has declined as shrub fields matured beyond the reach of wintering elk and timber reclaimed some of the burned areas. The carrying capacity of the habitat for elk has declined and elk numbers have followed.

To further complicate attempts to determine the carrying capacity of a particular habitat is the fact that bottlenecks, called limiting factors in bio-speak, occur. This is particularly true with migratory species such as mule deer. At one end of their range, habitat may be so abundant that one is left to wonder why more mule deer are not using it. The answer may lie at the other end of the migration where the average carrying capacity may be much lower. That population can never exceed the lowest value of "K" for the habitat in shortest supply. The limiting factor can be the groceries on winter or summer range, security cover, or even a smaller bottleneck such as fawning habitat, migration stopover habitat, or a combination of several limiting factors. For the Clearwater elk, forage was the bottleneck, not forest cover.

It is often difficult to really nail down carrying capacity, but sometimes it is easy to recognize when it has been exceeded. For example, bison and elk grazing in Yellowstone National Park's Lamar Valley have dramatically impacted habitat there, resulting in lost aspen and cottonwood regeneration, trampled stream banks, and overgrazed grasses, a clear degradation of habitat signaling that K has been exceeded.

There is a human social carrying capacity as well. There are just certain things humans won't tolerate from wild animals. Elk wintering among cattle feedlots is unacceptable, and if feedlots are an integral part of the carrying capacity, populations may need to be curtailed to match natural habitat. How many blackbirds we allow to share our world may be far lower than the number the habitat, which of course includes ripe grain fields, can support.

We may never be able to define what the carrying capacity of an area truly is for many animal species. It's a variable target that adjusts with conditions.

One thing is sure though: for the vast majority of species, carrying capacity, whatever it may be, is likely to diminish as habitat continues to shrink in quality and quantity.

Dormancy

Thousands of snow geese circled like a dervish over the marsh, landing once almost as a single organism, only to rise up again, their wings beating with a steady thunder. They had passed this way last fall as they retreated from winter's steadily increasing onslaught at their northern summer home. But now they were anxious to be about their business in the far north and the thawing pond ice opened their path like watery stepping stones—New Mexico, Utah, Idaho, Montana, British Columbia, Arctic.

As I walked along the dikes and dunes around the marsh, I wondered about the plants; the rushes and cattails, the grasses and flowers, and the shrubs and trees. They, too, were faced with overwhelming winter conditions.

But they could not simply make for warmer climes. Instead, they had to adopt a reliable strategy that would protect them from winter's bite but allow quick recovery once winter faded. Evolving an ability to go dormant, to suspend growth, was a prudent approach.

Dormancy has one caveat: waking up isn't an option. Triggers need to be consistent and reliable—not too soon and not too late. It is a delicate equation between a plant's internal chemistry and lengthening and warming days that finally nudges flowers or shrubs or trees from their winter's nap. If a January thaw can fool a plant into reactivating before winter is really gone, the plant may die when the chill returns.

Growth-inhibiting chemicals balance that equation. They are synthesized during the fall and stored in cells, shutting down growth before winter. Through the course of winter, their potency declines at a steady rate, finally dropping below the effective dose only after spring has arrived.

Reinitiating growth even just a little too early in the spring leaves plants susceptible to a sudden frost that can devastate the buds needed to form branches, leaves or fruit. My apricot trees were caught when a warm week in late March was followed by a week of subfreezing nights. The west half of the trees, the side facing the sun, woke up and that entire half of each tree was killed.

Natural selection has trusted that the earth's orbit around the sun, its spin, and its tilt are dependable constants in this world and has built another part of the equation around these facts. When the days begin to lengthen sufficiently, it is safe to awaken. Again, chemistry to the rescue. When daylight shines long enough, it initiates new reactions that cause buds to stretch, yawn and begin to push from the waxy bud scales that have protected them all winter.

Temperature plays a role as well. When valley aspen are in full bloom, those in the foothills are still slumbering. Soil and air temperatures are the final part of the equation and must be in tolerable range before growth reinitiates. Higher elevations mean shorter growing seasons because even though the photoperiod is the same as the valleys, temperatures are not and plants have to adapt.

The geese and the plants have evolved two very different ways of coping with the same environmental stress. For the birds, the world awakens and they respond. The plants are the world for most species though. And when they slip from dormancy, the world is right once again.

It Takes A Lot To Be Cool

I hadn't seen the rattlesnake curled up in the shade provided by the large rusty bucket when I reached in to remove the piece of litter. My hand was close enough for a strike but the snake didn't even raise its head. It was a scorcher of a day and it wouldn't take much excitement for that rattler's body temperature to rise into the lethal range. We stared at each other for a moment and then I slowly withdrew my hand. That bucket was one piece of trash that could just stay where it was.

Heat can be as life-threatening to wildlife as sub-zero winter temperatures, and staying cool during the hottest days of summer is challenging. Animals handle high summer temperatures in two basic ways: by behavioral choices and through physical adaptations.

Escaping the heat is sometimes the easiest thing an animal can do. Some, like the rattlesnake, seek shady areas out of direct sun. Big game animals like elk and deer may seek the thickest timber on north facing slopes. Many smaller mammals, reptiles, and amphibians retreat into underground burrows when the sun begins to climb. Some rodents are even clever enough to plug the burrows to maintain a more even temperature.

You will see fewer ground squirrels as summer progresses because they give up on beating the heat and just sleep it off. This strategy is called estivation, not unlike hibernation, but its purpose is to avoid the heat, not the lean months of winter. Only a few mammals estivate, but it is fairly common among snails, crabs, and amphibians.

Everyone knows that a panting dog is one trying to cool off through evaporation by moving air across a large wet tongue. Other animals employ a similar technique. Alligators will sit with mouths wide open and take advantage of air flows to draw off heat. Owls and nighthawks will also gape open-mouthed and rapidly flap their throats to evaporate moisture in their mouths.

As for the physical adaptations, many species of mammals shed warm winter coats for thinner summer coats. The summer coats provide less insulation allowing body heat to dissipate.

Long appendages are also a physical adaptation to beat the heat. For instance, the large ears of jackrabbits act like biological radiators, relieving heat quickly through blood veins close to the bare skin of the ears. This is often called Allen's Rule. And, according to the rule, the hotter the climate, the larger the ears, even in the same species.

Animals in hotter climates are often lighter in color than their more temperate relatives (called Gloger's Rule) and while there are many exceptions, it is easy to see that lighter coloration would be a benefit when it is hot.

There are some unique strategies too. For instance, the African lungfish burrows into the bottom of the lake bed and encases itself in a mucus coating to withstand the dry season, while vultures, which are dark-colored and thus susceptible to heat stress, urinate on their bare legs to cool the blood in the surface veins. This cooler blood is returned to the body for overall thermal regulation. Kangaroos lick their forearms to create evaporative cooling.

No matter how it is done, one thing is for sure: even in the animal world, it takes a lot of work to be cool.

Mountain Weather

The east facing ridge behind Bear Valley Lake in the Lemhi Mountains west of Leadore is high and rugged. Stunted pines have found a toehold in a few places, but for the most part, the bowl-shaped ridge is all scree and cliffs with persistent snow still enduring in deep crevasses. Even in August, a cornice hangs far over a steep face, its lip extending well beyond the edge of the slope.

This is a classic cirque basin, gouged and formed by a glacier thousands of years ago. Rock from the ridge was pushed ahead of the glacier and the terminal moraine it forms corrals the lake waters. The lake fits so tightly against the base of the ridge that most of the western sky, where storms build, is obscured from the lake shore.

My son and daughter and I dropped our packs at the calm edge of Bear Valley Lake (#1) about noon, happy for the break after a three hour climb. We swatted a few mosquitoes and stretched out on large boulders to rest. From our perspective at the lake, the sun was the only occupant of the cloudless blue sky and we now enjoyed the heat that had just moments before been making our hike uncomfortably warm.

Shortly though, a breeze rattled off the surrounding peaks, slid down the mountain and began to ruffle the lake. We couldn't see any change, but this seemed to be an omen of an approaching storm. The lake's mirror surface was replaced at first by small riffles, then, as the breeze revved up to a decided wind, riffles turned to whitecaps and waves slapped the shoreline. We donned jackets, built a fire behind a boulder and looked anxiously at the sky. Dark and ominous clouds roiled over the ridge like a boiling cauldron. Rain and lightning were sure to follow.

We weren't too worried for our safety; we were well prepared and in a reasonably safe location but I did wonder if this was a harbinger for the next three days. I have been on rainsoaked backpacking trips before and didn't count them among my favorite experiences.

The rain finally began to fall shortly after we set up camp. We cooked dinner and fought the weather for awhile, but I finally crawled in my tent early and went to sleep to the sound of rain on the nylon. Somewhere around 5 a.m., the rain stopped, but water continued to drip from trees overhanging our campsite. When the dripping stopped, we arose to a beautiful, if soggy morning.

But like the previous day, dark clouds built up again in the afternoon, obscuring the sun and bouncing ominous thunder off the granite peaks. Rain erased the mirror reflections off the lake, but skies were clear again by morning.

Rain in the mountains, especially afternoon showers, is to be expected. Only the foolish venture there without some sort of rain protection and a smattering of skill to deal with a downpour. The prudent will even take a peek at the weather forecast in advance, but will look slightly askance at any forecast that calls for clear skies. Sometimes those clear skies are awfully wet as the mountains seem to be able to manufacture their own weather.

Mountain rain seems to be a paradigm for life. Rain happens—it is often unpredictable, frequently inconvenient, and sometimes the results can be catastrophic. All we can do is be as prepared as possible, hunker down if necessary, and hope for a hole in the clouds.

Snow Drifts

While driving home from work last week, a restless south wind sent snow skittering like smoke across the highway. The moving snow and leaden skies made the world outside the car seem inhospitable indeed. Already, tongues of drifts were growing behind each and every object that blocked the wind. Experience told me that if it kept up, driving this same road in the morning would be a challenging experience.

I thought back on a Christmas morning half a dozen years previous. My wife was trying to get home from night shift at the hospital but our usual artery home was blocked with a hundreds-of-yards-long drift up to six feet deep. I sent her another way, but that, too, was blocked—at least for a car. I jumped in the four wheel drive and blazed a trail to her. We abandoned the car until the snowplows could open the road.

Wind-drifted snow shapes the winter landscape like an artist. Sometimes the sculpting is rhythmic, like waves on a sea. More often, the designs are unique. Always, the results are impressive—sometimes massive and often catastrophic for transportation.

Over the course of a winter, wind-drifted snow changes our world many times. With a few inches of new snow and a stiff wind, landscapes transform overnight. A steady wind deposits and re-deposits snow like a musician working out a tune.

Drifting snow may not be on par with a natural disaster such as an earthquake, tornado, or a flood, but our world still rocks wherever wind and snow sing their dolce duet. In the past several weeks getting just about anywhere on the Snake River Plain has been difficult, mainly because of wind-driven snow. Snowmobile has been the best mode of travel on many county roads.

Drift accumulation is not as haphazard as it looks. Snow moves with the air currents until an object such as a tree, a fence, or a house, interrupts the wind. The final score is influenced by changes to the physical world that dictate where drifts will form and where the snow will come from. For example, fallowed fields don't hold snow as well as grain stubble. And, when the landscape gets re-arranged by new activities such as construction, wind drifting patterns change and can create fresh and sometimes nasty surprises.

Drifting occurs on the lee side of an object. If that object is permeable, like a picket fence, and the cadence of the wind slows, but doesn't stop, the snow begins to drop out as wind velocity declines and a drift begins. That is the principle of a snow fence. The best snow fences are not all solid but rather, about 50% solid and 50% open. Wind passes through the fence and loses steam, dropping its snow on the back side.

Behind a snow fence, a drift reaches a crescendo when it is about as tall as the fence and about ten times the height in length. Once it has reached this equilibrium, additional storms will pass right over it, looking for the next obstacle.

Like a piano note, flying snow doesn't go on forever. When we feel the stinging ice particles of a blizzard, it is tempting to think that they came from Montana and are headed for Utah or vice versa. That may be the direction it is traveling, but research has shown that a snowflake or ice granule is evaporating as it is driven by the wind. A flake or granule won't make it five miles before it completely evaporates.

In some places in the West, snow drift management is an important issue, and not just for traffic safety. A lot of water can be captured for wildlife and livestock use throughout the summer if drifts are created in the appropriate locations.

Snow drifts. Sometimes they can be a real hassle, occasionally dangerous as they impact transportation. They are also part of the character of winter, sculpting shapes as lovely as any artist could create. Do you love 'em or hate 'em? Actually, I find that I do both.

Good Dads

In Nature, dads get a lot of bad press. Much of it is deserved. After all, killing your rivals' offspring is reprehensible in the human world. Males of many species are also promiscuous and parentally irresponsible. They may mate with dozens of females and then participate not one wit in the raising of the resultant offspring, preferring instead to hang out with the boys, the same ones who were recently rivals.

But that isn't always the case. Many males are devoted mates and fathers. They defend their mate, help her raise the babies, and are protective of their young. A hissing male goose protecting his brood with wings outstretched and a male lion defending his pride garner respect for all dads.

To prove my point, I spent a little time in a blind observing a pair of robins and their two offspring. I came away convinced that not all wild dads are bad examples.

It was natural for the female robin to be dedicated to her eggs and chicks. She brooded them, used her body to protect them from the rain and wind. The male though, was right beside her all the way, from building the nest to raising the chicks, and I was impressed with his diligence.

When brooding the eggs became nearly a full time job for the female, the male robin hunted, not just for himself, but for his mate as well. He demonstrated marvelous restraint and commitment when he came back with worms or caterpillars rather than devour them himself. Often it was not just one caterpillar, but several at a time firmly clamped in his beak. When he fed her, there appeared to be emotion there (forgive my anthropomorphism) that went beyond instinctual. It seemed like, if not love, then caring and tenderness.

When the eggs hatched, the female ate pieces of the blue eggshell she picked up, presumably to replace the calcium she lost in laying the eggs. The male did house cleaning though, carrying remaining eggshell pieces well away from the nest.

On Father's Day, he was busy all day, hunting and helping to care for the chicks. During the time I watched him, he averaged a return to the nest about every ten minutes. The chicks would instantly awake and beg for the food they knew he offered. He took a turn at sitting on the nest while his mate took a break, and he even participated in removing the chicks' feces—the robin equivalent to cleaning toilets—again to keep the nest clean.

He is protective of his babies and intolerant of other male robins close to the nest. The big guy with the camera is okay, but not these interlopers. He chases them with a vengeance, squawking his displeasure.

I don't know if all robin dads are this attentive—after all, I have a sample size of one. He sets an excellent example of diligence and devotion, though.

With only one fledgling left in my own nest, I contemplated my own role as a father. Did I match up to this simple little bird? Did I fulfill my role as a father to the best of my ability? Those are sobering questions as I begin my new role as grandfather.

Winter Tracking

Readin' sign, telling about an animal's movements by tracks, droppings or other signs of its passage was once an integral and essential frontier skill. Knowing what an animal was up to, its mood, or where it might be headed, often meant the difference between eating meat or shoe leather. Nowadays, however, it is the rare person who can tell one track from another, much less divine what the animal was doing when it made the tracks.

That is what makes winter such a good field season. Equipped with a field guide on tracks and a desire to unravel the mysteries of winter, countless hours can be spent learning and observing animal movements in the snowy medium regardless of the time of day. You may learn things not obvious even with the observation of the animal itself.

A single set of tracks lacing across a fresh snow can recount the nightlong story of one animal's struggle to survive. However, after a few days, the accumulation of tracks can reveal patterns and haunts. The story doesn't always unravel easily, but solving the riddle will stretch the naturalist in you. It can be the ultimate naturalist experience to accurately discern facts about wildlife from the clues they leave.

When I am hunting sign, the tracks of a mouse are as interesting as those of a deer. The mouse obviously found something so important in its wanderings that it was worth the exposure to death from a furred or feathered predator. Just what was all the scurrying about? Was it a primal search for food or hunting for a potential mate? Or, perhaps mice just get bored too and it was out on a walkabout, checking out the neighborhood.

Reading sign is much more than simply tracking an animal to its destination. It is like the script of a movie, frozen for a time in the snow, the why and the wherefore written in white for you to divine. I once came upon a fresh fawn mule deer carcass, its blood still staining the snow. From the carcass two bloody-beaked golden eagles reluctantly fled. Since this fawn had not been dead when I had passed by several hours previous, I determined to ascertain, if I could, the story of its fate.

I did not have far to go. The fawn had slid 50 bloodless yards down a snowy hill like an unconscious tobogganer. Yet, even steady tracks wandered from sagebrush to sagebrush to the beginning of the slide—obviously an unconcerned fawn catching an afternoon snack. The attack had been sudden, unheralded and ruthlessly effective. With no other tracks to add to the case, the conclusion was obvious: the eagles had struck the deer down, leaving eagle sign in that airy realm I could not see.

An astute naturalist will look for more than just prints. The length of the stride and the dimensions and depth of the print can reveal the species, size, and sometimes the sex of the animal. A perceptive observer may note that the urine hole of a bull elk enters the snow at a different angle than a cow. An adult male wolf lifts a leg while subordinate males and females squat to urinate. An animal with a purpose will often travel in a straight line while a feeding animal or one looking for a bed will wander or even circle. Paying attention to detail is the hallmark of a good naturalist.

Reading sign tells you more about the animal than just its species. Once, while following a group of elk in fresh shallow snow, I was baffled for a few moments by the unusual circular holes on either side of one set of tracks. After a brief head scratching, I realized that I was looking at the tracks of a bull and the round holes were marks left by his antlers when he bent his neck for a bite of grass.

Fear and ambition can be written in the sign as well. Jackrabbit tracks spaced up to nine feet apart in a punctuated twisting line through the sagebrush may indicate a rabbit fleeing for its life. Coyote tracks similarly spaced in leaps and bounds along the rabbit path reflect an enterprising canine with a taste for rabbit. The story remains long after the drama has ended. Unravel the sign to its end to see if fate favored the coyote's dinner or the rabbit's survival in the final chapter of the tale.

You will find sign to read virtually everywhere from your backyard to the canal bank to the fields and river shores. So the next time you feel like a good mystery, drop the remote and put on your parka!

CHAPTER 3

WILDLIFE

Marsh Wrens

I met him last spring. He was just half an ounce, but it was all attitude. He had a territory to defend and a large human wasn't going to keep him from his rounds as he sped from cattail to cattail, climbing each and belting out his song of challenge from the fluffy tops.

Easily recognized as a wren by the jaunty, almost arrogant 90 degree angle of his tail arching over his back, his home revealed his full identity as a marsh wren. Marshes are his exclusive habitat, and the way he acted, his alone to rule.

He sang almost incessantly. My Sibley bird guide said that his song should be a, "gurgling, rattling trill with distinctive musical and mechanical quality." Such attempts to describe birdsong in human terms rarely satisfy. Gurgling? Rattling? This much I knew: my bird's song wasn't musical; in fact, it grated on my nerves just a little. Sibley went on to say that the male Western marsh wren may know a hundred songs so maybe today was just rap music day.

I admired his ferocious energy. A scrappy streetfighter, he furiously attacked any other male that entered his territory as he raced from one end to the other. He even eyed me several times, rattling out his challenge and scolding me. But apparently he decided I was too ugly to interest any female marsh wrens, and I was subsequently ignored.

The marsh wren is accused of being plain, even homely. Nonetheless, I found him handsome enough. True, the marsh wren, male or female, is mostly mottled browns with just the hint of fashion in the barred tail and whitish eye stripe. A long, thin, and slightly curved bill is the only stylish accoutrement. But spirit counts for something and he was a joy to watch so my mind's eye saw him differently.

A willingness to fight aside, there is a brutish side to this male as well. That long thin bill, perfect for picking invertebrates from the plants and even from beneath the surface of the marsh, is also the devil's tool. Males routinely enter nests of rival pairs and plunge that bill into the eggs or even the flesh of the young. And not just other marsh wrens are at risk. Male marsh wrens consider all other birds as competitors and deal ruthlessly with their young. For them, it's bird against bird, survival of the fittest.

Despite his shortcomings, I admire my little friend. He is fully committed to his duties and has seemingly endless energy and enthusiasm. He takes full advantage of every minute, really living.

Mostly though, I admire the way he sings. In a time where many die with their music still in them, he sings with the gusto of a pirate. He holds nothing back, caring not at all what the world thinks of his music; rattled, gurgled, trilled, or otherwise. And in that, he teaches a grand lesson: even if your song is off-key or lacks harmony or rhythm, sing it anyway. It is the only way to live.

Love of Wildlife

For our daughter-in-law, Laura, a recent transplant from California, seeing a moose was her number one outdoor priority, and she had been thwarted at every step. She and her husband, our son Ben, spent the summer trying to see a moose in the wilds of Island Park and on the Snake River, to no avail. Right place, wrong time seemed to be their motto.

So, when alerted by my wife to a moose just one mile from our home, Laura raced from Rigby to Ucon. After a fruitless summer of searching the South Fork, Henry's Fork and Island Park, her wish was fulfilled when she saw her first moose within suburbia. She called me to report that it was the biggest moose on earth and she was forever indebted to Cathy.

I smiled at her youthful enthusiasm and appreciation for the opportunity. It was a great initiation into what I hope will become a lifetime love for all things wild. I was certainly surprised, though, when a friend, one who has trodden this earth even longer than I have, reported that this same bull was the first live moose he had ever seen. It reminded me that we often take the benefits of living here for granted.

During Bullwinkle's day-long tenure in our neighborhood, a steady stream of people made the pilgrimage to see him. An excited, Yellowstone-like atmosphere, something between a shrine and a carnival, permeated the air as people talked in hushed tones and warned their kids not to get too close.

It was gratifying to see so many people make an effort to share this experience. It proved that wildlife is still a valued commodity in our area. Oh, I'm sure that novelty played a part, and it was probably just a curiosity to some, like a visit to a free zoo. I like to believe though, that it went deeper than that for most people. It was a fleeting call to the primal appeal of nature that quietly stirs inside everyone. It was a *link* to our roots, to the undercurrent called nature that so often gets buried under the tonnage of civilized life. They were answering that call, however briefly and out of context.

My great fear, though, is that our instinctual need for contact with nature may slowly become satiated with brief civilized wildlife encounters and fascinating nature programs on TV. Will the glitter of technology one day supplant our need for real nature? The book, <u>Last Child in the Woods/Nature Deficit Disorder</u>, by Richard Louv, chillingly describes that the connection our kids naturally feel toward the natural world is quickly fading in a world increasingly filled with electronic distractions. He also documents the serious impact this is having on their lives.

In <u>A Sand County Almanac</u>, Aldo Leopold declared,

> There are some who can live without wild things, and some who cannot. ...Like winds and sunsets, wild things were taken for granted until progress began to do away with them. Now we face the question whether a still higher 'standard of living' is worth its cost in things natural, wild, and free. For us of the minority, the opportunity to see geese is more important than television, and the chance to find a pasque-flower is a right as inalienable as free speech.

I suspect that for many Idahoans, wild things and the land upon which they depend are intricately woven into our "standard of living", a second paycheck, so to speak. We will need to work hard to keep these wild threads from unraveling with our kids.

Best of the Best

Sometimes entering the record book is a matter of accident, being in the wrong place at the right time. Such was the case of flight attendant Vesna Vulovic who survived a fall from 33,000 feet when the DC-9 jet she was in exploded. Or, park ranger Roy Sullivan, who survived seven separate lightning strikes over 35 years.

Often the desire to enter the record books and somehow earn a degree of immortality is so strong that people will do all manner of things—Benjamin Drucker set a record when he had 745 18-gauge surgical needles inserted into his body in 2 hr 21 minutes—just to be the BEST at something.

I thought it might be interesting to review a few of the best of the best in the animal world (according to the Guinness Book of World Records) where being the best actually means something.

Fastest land mammal: It is no surprise that the cheetah of Africa holds this record. The official record is 64.3 mph over a short distance. However, our own pronghorn antelope holds the record for fastest sustained speeds: 55 mph over half a mile and 35 mph over four miles.

Fastest Bird: Peregrine falcons have long been recognized as the fastest birds in the air with recorded dive speeds clocked up to 217 mph. However, on the ground the peregrine is nothing when compared to the ostrich (which also is the world's largest bird). Despite being 300 pounds and 8 feet tall, an ostrich can move across the savannas at 45 mph. And, if they choose not to run, watch out—they are reported to be able to kick a hole through a car door!

Highest Flying Bird: On November 29, 1973, a Ruppell's vulture collided with a commercial jet—at 37,000 feet! Mt. Everest, by comparison, juts 29,035 feet into the sky.

Longest Snake: The reticulated python of southeast Asia, Indonesia, and the Philippines regularly exceeds 20 feet. The record length is 32 feet 9.5 inches, for a specimen shot in Celebes, Indonesia, in 1912. Think of that the next time a three foot long rattler stops your heart.

Largest Mammal: Hands down the largest mammal, largest animal and largest animal ever to inhabit this planet (the largest dinosaurs discovered in the last several decades still don't top it) is the blue whale. Even calves begin life at up to three tons and adults reach 100 feet and 130 tons. There is a record of a female caught in 1947 that weighed 190 tons and stretched 90 feet and another even larger one caught in 1909 that measured 110 feet. The largest land mammal, the African elephant, is puny by comparison: the largest on record is 12.24 tons.

Tallest mammal: No surprise here—the giraffe of Africa is the tallest mammal on the planet. The average maximum height is 18 feet, but George, a transplant from Kenya to the Chester Zoo in England, was 19 feet tall. Incidentally, giraffes have no more neck vertebrae than we do (seven) they are just a lot longer.

Drucker's needles do little to impress me, but I have to admit that contemplating a bird flying with the jet liners or a whale bigger than a tractor-trailer rig fires my imagination.

Best of the Best Part 2

Our family went to see the much acclaimed movie, *The Chronicles of Narnia: The Lion, the Witch, and the Wardrobe,* based on the novel of the same name by C.S. Lewis. An impressive movie with a wonderful storyline, but it left me slightly unnerved. It is not that I can't take the action—it is that this movie, like so many in the past ten years, seems to be bent on creating more and wilder special effects than any predecessors.

I realize that the books the movies are based on often contain wild imaginings, but seeing them on screen, often in surreal settings, creates an audience that is very hard to impress without—MORE. The result, in my mind, is that our senses are dulled to real things that truly are amazing. Kids visit zoos and come away unimpressed because real animals just don't stack up to the movie versions; the zoo's lion can't hold a candle to Narnia's digital Aslan. In short, our dazzle button is getting harder to push and we seem to be losing respect for things in the real world.

For example, it is truly amazing that the blue whale is not only the largest animal on the planet, but it is also the loudest. The song of the blue whale, belted out at an incredible 188 decibels, may be heard for many miles under the ocean and may last for up to 10 hours (The loudest human, on the other hand, Jill Drake, London, 2000, screamed a mere 129 decibels, while a jet aircraft reaches only 140 decibels). The songs of blue whales are truly magnificent, but can they compete with talking lions and centaurs on the silver screen?

In 1987, scientists documented a leatherback sea turtle, the largest of the sea turtles, diving to a depth of 3,973 feet below the surface of the ocean off the West Indies. I might remind you that a mile is 5,280 feet so this dive was three-quarters of a mile deep. It held its breath, survived the tremendous cold and pressure of the deep, and returned to the surface—that is seriously impressive. And we need to remember, this was a record only because it is not every day that leatherback turtle dives are measured. For all we know, this could be fairly routine. Nonetheless, sword fighting rodents make the leatherback's true to life achievement seem boring.

Or, take the case of the Fierce Snake (or Inland Taipan) of Australia. This snake has the most toxic venom of any snake. Maximum yield recorded (for one bite) is 110mg. That would probably be enough to kill over 100 people. Yet a fairy tale witch with an evil wand could turn enemies to stone. Pretty tough competition.

The Arctic tern makes an annual migration of 20,000 miles from the Arctic to the Antarctic and back again each year and may fly 1.5 million miles in a lifetime of migration. This journey must be fraught with perils and adventures that would make great reality TV. But time travel and fourth and fifth dimensions are far more exciting.

Animals do so many things that are fascinating and amazing that we really shouldn't need Hollywood attempts to make them better. Enjoy the fairy tales and the adventures, but I hope we can keep separate the workings of computer animation and the true life wonders of the natural world.

Deer Tales

The following story is true. Hard to believe, but true. Last week, a convoy of pickup trucks from Idaho Falls rushed through a hot Wyoming afternoon, headed toward a youth activity east of the continental divide. The last truck pulled a beautiful 26 foot fiberglass camp trailer.

Coming down the far side of South Pass at about 55 mph, the driver of the last truck saw a brown flash in his rear view mirror and heard a thump. His next glance in the mirror revealed a large hole in the left front of the trailer, emphasis on large. He pulled over and searched both shoulders of the highway for nearly half a mile to find what he had hit. He found no carcasses, no roadside trash that could have made the hole in the trailer.

By the time he got back to the truck and trailer, the other two rigs had turned around and their drivers were staring at the gaping hole. Their question, "What did you hit?" was answered with a quizzical shrug from the returning driver.

After considerable speculation, they determined that, as illogical as it sounded, whatever the driver had hit must be inside the trailer. They opened the front door and cautiously stepped inside, thoughts of Chris Farley's *Tommy Boy* swirling in their heads. Like *Tommy Boy*, if whatever had gone through the trailer wall was a living creature, there was a chance it was still alive and sporting a severe case of attitude.

A look into the damaged bedroom proved that the victim was indeed a living creature for there was a little hair and blood smeared on the inside edge of the hole.

The three men collectively scratched their heads: in this case they had expected to find the miscreant in a tangled mess on the queen sized bed. Instead, they spotted the culprit when they looked through the bedroom door and down the narrow hall to the back of the trailer.

Resting on her back in eternal peace on the couch at the far end of the trailer was a yearling doe mule deer. With all four feet in the air, she was wrapped around a completely unscathed drum set. Between her and the hole in the front of the trailer was a path of destruction that included the thermostat, television and table.

How the deer came to rest on the couch sprawled out like she was ready for the next soap opera became a topic of energetic discussion for the three men. Two likely theories emerged: First that the deer had staggered in a panic toward the back of the moving trailer and died, either from injuries or fright, as she reached the end of the trap. The second theory was that the deer was killed on impact but ricocheted around the inside of the trailer like a cannonball with the laws of physics dictating her final resting place.

Regardless how the deer ended up so comfortably on the couch, I have taken a few lessons from this experience. First, trailers aren't as sturdy as they appear to be. Second, deer are tougher than they appear to be. Third, there are some animals that should be removed from the gene pool as quickly as possible. And fourth, truth truly is often stranger than fiction.

From Eagles to Gulls

I had taken a day off work and driven 200 miles to photograph bald eagles at Farmington Bay on the Great Salt Lake. Each year, dozens of eagles concentrate there around mid-February and it was reported that this was a banner year.

Several dozen cars were ahead of me as I drove down the seriously potholed road of the waterfowl management area. Everywhere, lenses just smaller than the Hubble telescope protruded from windows and sat perched on tripods.

However, when I deployed my own used-car priced lens, I found a nasty surprise—I couldn't see anything. I had tripped over the lens while loading the car, and that minor incident was obviously more serious than I had thought.

For several hours, I rounded up tools and fought to salvage my trip. No good. The repair was beyond my very rudimentary skill and the lens was destined for a trip back home to Nikon.

It is rare when my ability to take a day off coincides with an event worthy of photographing and I was bummed. I debated what to do, contemplating just heading home and feeling sorry for myself.

Finally though, I decided to poke around Farmington Bay Waterfowl Management Area with the last couple of hours of daylight. After a tooth-jarring ride down to the end of the pothole-cratered road, I sat and sulked, as the eagles were far too distant to photograph with my remaining lens. With nothing better to do, I began to closely observe some gulls loitering around a small island of open water.

There were ring-billed and California gulls in plumages from yearling to adult. Handsome enough, but both are common and certainly not as photogenic as the majestic bald eagle. They quickly grew used to my presence though, and went about their business as if I wasn't there. Despite my sour attitude, I soon found myself intrigued by their antics.

Unlike the eagles that sat for hours perched boringly in a tree, the gulls were constantly active. They rotated through a pattern of landing on the thin ice near shore, wading into the water and then taking flight. Each time one would land, a squabble ensued as it jostled into position on the ice. Wings spread, beak agape, and emitting a horrendous noise, the newcomer would win its spot and peace quickly returned. Like a high school cafeteria, the social interaction was endlessly complicated..

A pair of northern harriers worked the area and, seemingly just for fun, soared low over the gulls. Pandemonium. Every gull took wing with a cacophony of terrified squawks. They circled for a moment and then, several at a time, dropped back to earth and resumed life as a gull.

Frequently, from a few feet above the water, a gull would hover, twist, and with wings tucked back, plunge headfirst into the water. Several times one was rewarded with small fish.

The time passed quickly as I watched and photographed. The gulls had turned my frustration into fascination and I forgot about eagles, expensive failed gear, and wasted days.

When the light failed, I headed north. The potholes made for slow going and gave me time to contemplate. The broken lens had changed my day, but hadn't ruined it. Opportunity is often born of catastrophe. It took a flock of ordinary noisy gulls to teach me that.

Yellow Jackets Must Die!

Next to my computer sits a can of hornet and wasp killer, the kind that has 20% more than the original. It is resting benignly right now, but soon it will fulfill its purpose and spread death from up to 20 feet away. I will wield it without mercy in a war where no prisoners will be taken.

My attitude toward yellow jacket wasps, those pesky little picnic ruining flying stingers, began in earnest last week. I was calmly weeding in my flowers, dressed in baggy shorts and a t-shirt. Without warning and without provocation, a yellow jacket shot up my shorts and a dagger-like searing pain radiated from the back of my leg, about mid thigh.

I fought to keep the yellow jacket from proceeding further up my leg where permanent damage could occur and looked down to discover half a dozen more swarming me. I cleared the patio bench behind me like an Olympic vaulter but not before I was stung twice more, once on each forearm. I did a little dance in my backyard (the purpose of which should now be clear to any neighbors who happened to be watching) before I rid myself of the ill-tempered attackers.

Less than a week previous, I had been stung on the arm by a yellow jacket that was apparently intent on bagging a trophy. It landed on my arm and without a second's hesitation, plunged its stinger in deep and released its toxins. Worse, it flew out of reach before I could react, probably expecting to see me choke and die any second.

Last summer, I was stung no less than three separate times. Perhaps I built up an intolerance to the stings because this time it was painful enough I lost sleep and swelled up until thighs and forearms resembled cherry pies.

And, I know of worse. A friend was having a pre-wedding summer party and took a drink from her soda only to have the yellow jacket lurking inside the can sting her on the lip! Needless to say, the wedding the next day proceeded without a photographer. Another friend nearly died from anaphylactic shock when he had an allergic reaction to a yellow jacket sting.

During summer, we all have to be on our guard against yellow jackets. Hives will grow from a single queen in the springtime to up to several thousand wasps by late summer. Watch for hives in holes and crevices in the ground, in bricks, piles of wood, and just about anywhere else they can fly into.

Yellow jackets are attracted to anything sweet, so keep food at picnics covered until the last moment. Tight fitting trash can lids will also help. Avoid wearing perfumes and bright clothing when in yellow jacket country, which seems to be just about anywhere. Yellow jacket traps are effective but you may need a lot of them.

I suppose that as a nature columnist, I should try to understand yellow jackets and point out how much they serve the environment as pollinators and natural cleanup crews and actually improve our lives. I should try to schmooze readers with some kind of drivel about "live and let live", or, "if you don't bother them they won't bother you," but while the former would be true, the latter would be lies.

When it comes to vicious stinging insects that attack without provocation or cause, I feel no compulsion to be patient, enduring, understanding, or forgiving. It is war and I am headed for their villages where I will spare neither hive nor offspring!

Know Thy Enemy

Despite my fondest dreams, it is, alas, unrealistic to even fantasize about the global extermination of yellow jacket wasps. One study estimates that even if 99.9% of all the yellow jacket queens were destroyed in one spring, the 0.1% would still be enough to repopulate their habitat without much more than a blip in their population curve.

I doubt I can ever conquer my loathing for a flying stinger with a bad temper but, since I can't eliminate yellow jackets, I suppose the next best thing is to *know my enemy*.

Yellow jackets are part of the Family Vespidae, which also includes paper wasps and hornets. They all have narrow waists (very apparent in the paper wasp—less so in the yellow jacket), round legs, and are relatively hairless. All can retain their stingers and sting multiple times. Equally annoying, wasps, especially yellow jackets, also bite hard enough to feel like a sting. Given their propensity to consume carrion, these bites can cause serious infections.

Wasps are often confused with bees (honey bees and bumblebees), but there are some very big differences. One of the most important differences is food habits. Bees feed on nectar and pollen and have flattened hind legs to carry pollen back to the hive. Wasps, on the other hand, are predators, preying on other insects, spiders, humans, and the like. They are considered very beneficial (you knew I had to say that somewhere) because of all the insects they destroy. Yellow jackets also search out anything sweet or dead and are part of Nature's carrion cleanup crew. Without carrion eaters, we would have died out long ago from diseases bred in rotting corpses.

Bees build their hives from wax and may use the hive for years. Wasps on the other hand, build their nests from a papery substance they make from chewing wood and leaves and do not reuse nests. Paper wasps build their nests on exposed surfaces and the rearing chambers are exposed. But yellow jackets prefer to build inside existing holes. If they build outside, the nest is completely covered with the papery product so the rearing cells are not exposed at all. The classic nest that looks like an oversized football is usually the work of the bald-faced hornet, not a wasp.

The wasp life cycle begins in the spring when fertilized queens emerge from their winter hiding places in May or June. The queen immediately begins to lay eggs in a new nest site. She raises the first batch of female workers which then assume the tasks of increasing the size of the colony and caring for larvae and the queen. They feed the larvae with the insects they kill or the meat they scavenge. The colony may expand to 4,000 to 5,000 workers by late August. It is no wonder they can ruin a summer picnic!

There is probably only one thing that keeps wasps from taking over the world (and this is the exciting part); wasps only live for one season! All but the queens are killed by the frosts of autumn.

It is a somewhat hollow victory to realize that should I fail to kill any offending yellow jackets, Mother Nature will finish the job by November anyway. I am not likely to stop with my uncharitable vengeance though—I will just try to handle the disappointment.

Wild Horses

When the mare and foal topped the hill alongside the Spar Canyon Road near Challis, they were already on a dead run. Before I could do more than hit the brakes and exclaim the obvious, "wild horses!" they were across the road and down in the wash. Our first encounter with wild horses was over. My wife and I were both thrilled and amazed.

For some reason, I had envisioned wild horses as a scraggly, genetically inbred lot, hardly worth the grass they consumed. I was wrong. The mare was buckskin brown with flowing dark mane and tail that billowed as she ran. She was well muscled, sleek and beautiful. Junior was almost a carbon copy of his mother.

The wild horses that roam the West today are descended from domestic stock brought to North America by Europeans, especially the Spanish Conquistadors, beginning in the 1500s. The nucleus came from horses that escaped or were intentionally released. For example, during the Great Pueblo Revolt in 1680, thousands of horses were released from mission ranches. There is still a strong Spanish influence in populations with the longest histories of escaped horses. Later escapes included Thoroughbred, Morgan, Quarter Horse, and draft horses.

Since these horses are descendents of domestic stock, it is technically incorrect to call them wild. The proper term is feral. A housecat gone to the wild does not become a wild cat, it becomes a feral cat. So, technically these horses should be called feral horses.

It could be argued though, that these escaped horses are a re-introduction of native wildlife that was extirpated from this continent. The fossil record clearly indicates that the genus <u>Equus</u> evolved on the American Continent. From here they spread across the Bering land bridge to Asia, Europe, the Middle East, and Northern Africa. It was only sometime in the past 8,000 years that horses disappeared from the North American scene in some catastrophic event that pushed them to extinction.

So, although the horses that now roam free are descended from domesticated and selectively bred stock (as opposed to truly wild horses still roaming the Mongolian highlands), their deepest roots are already here. I will refer to them as wild horses.

Today, there are an estimated 25,000 wild horses in 178 herds spread across ten Western states. Nevada supports the most wild horses with an estimated population of 12,400. Wyoming runs a poor second with about 3,900 animals, California is third with about 2,900 animals.

Idaho has an estimated population of about 800 wild horses. There are six herd management units. The closest to our region is the Challis herd unit. You can look for wild horses in the canyons from Willow Creek Summit (between Mackay and Challis on Highway 93) to Challis.

Since wild horses have few predators, the Bureau of Land Management conducts routine round ups where excess animals are sold to qualified buyers. I once hired an outfitter who rode a large gelding that he had acquired from a wild horse auction. He said it was the best horse he had ever owned.

If you go searching for wild horses, remember one thing: although they come from domesticated ancestors, they are as wild as any elk, deer, or pronghorn and are very wary. Binoculars will be a great help.

Because of my misconceived notions about wild horses, they have never been on my "must see" list. My brief encounter has changed that and I look forward to my next opportunity.

A Tale of Wolves and Bears

Early one morning, up Soda Butte Creek in the LaMar Valley, six wolves were on the trail of a bull elk. As the chase ensued, the bull headed for the lower, more open country along the creek. But even running full speed, he could not shake his pursuers. He splashed into the creek and they tore at his haunches. He slipped on the wet stones and that was the mistake the wolves were waiting for. They forced him down and soon his blood was mingling with the waters of the creek.

The entire chase was recorded by an incredibly lucky videographer. But by the time we happened upon the scene, three of the pack had already eaten their fill and moved off into the timber to rest. Three others, a black and two grays, were resting there on the bank. From the obeisance the other wolves paid to the large gray one, we assumed it to be the Alpha male of the pack.

A coyote sauntered on the scene. Coyotes are a wolf's favorite toy and all of us (there were probably 75 onlookers) thought that the temerity of this coyote would get it killed. The wolves seemed to notice but must have been too full for a chase. The coyote made several aborted attempts down the bank toward the carcass, but finally it ran short of nerve and moved off.

One by one, the wolves moved off into the timber, disappearing like ghosts. Only the alpha male was left to guard the carcass, which he did laying on his side with his eyes closed. Watching a wolf sleep isn't tremendously entertaining, and the temptation to move on to search for other wildlife action was strong. We resisted the temptation though and stayed with the wolf. And we were glad we did. The action finally heated up at about 4:00 p.m. The grizzly we had seen about four miles downstream finally made it to the scene. He went straight to the carcass and began to feast. We were sure a rumble was about to begin, but the wolf did nothing. After an hour of steady feeding, the bear climbed onto the bank to rest. He was obviously aware of the wolf but seemed unconcerned.

Two top predators, one elk carcass. Neither bear nor wolf interested in sharing. A showdown seemed inevitable. And predictably, it was the wolf that started it. He rose, stretched and headed straight for the bear. There was considerable posturing on both accounts but it was obvious that the wolf was going to test the bear's resolve. Several times the bear moved down onto the carcass and stood on it with all four feet while the wolf watched from the bank. Finally though, they faced off and in a sudden rush of raised hackles, bared teeth, and growls, the grizzly pushed the wolf back and definitively claimed his status as king of the carcass.

Before dusk fell, several other wolves returned to find the carcass possessed by the demon bear. A smaller black one went through a similar dance that the Alpha male had done and even had the temerity to get close to the carcass, but to no avail. The bear roared off the bank in a fury and the wolf quickly retreated. The king was still king.

The entire saga lasted for over 13 hours. It was a show worth watching but like most of the drama nature has to offer, it demanded patience to remain on site during the long lulls. Had I been my normal impatient self or unprepared to stay for a long period, we would have missed an incredible show.

Roaming House Cats

After years of vehement opposition to having a cat for a pet, I finally succumbed when my son's friend presented him with a blue-eyed kitten we promptly named Tinkerbell. Tink, as we call her, has slowly wormed her way, if not into my heart, at least onto my chair and is becoming a part of the family. Our golden retriever is particularly fond of her and after a very rocky start, they are best friends.

Cats (Felis cattus) were first domesticated from wildcats in Egypt about 4,000 years ago. They were useful in controlling rodents and snakes but slowly become so popular that they were considered a form of deity. As the cats adjusted to a civilized life, they underwent many changes from their ancestors including pelt coloration, brain size (downsized), and intestine length (up-sized). They became truly domesticated.

But domesticated doesn't mean lacking in natural hunting instincts. Now that I have a cat, I have potentially become part of a nationwide problem. Pet cats allowed to roam freely outdoors become what biologists call subsidized predators.

Predators in a natural system kill to live. If prey is scarce, predator populations will decline. Subsidized predators, on the other hand, do not need to hunt to survive. Often, well fed house cats do not even eat their prey. They hunt even if prey is scarce, putting undue pressure on prey populations and competing with natural predators.

Pet cats not only kill exotic house mice (a pest) they also kill native mice, shrews and other mammals, to the tune of an estimated hundreds of millions a year. In addition, subsidized cat predation may actually fuel increased house mice. When *native* species decline, there is more room for the house mice to expand.

Then there are the birds. Native songbird populations are declining at an alarming rate. There are numerous reasons including habitat destruction and collisions with windows, windtowers, cell phone towers, and vehicles. Scientists with the U.S. Fish and Wildlife Service estimated though, that pet cats may kill 100 million or more birds annually, and are a serious threat to songbirds. They also become direct competitors with native predators such as owls and have been found to impact conservation efforts on some imperiled bird species.

The most recent research attached miniature video cameras to housecats and found that the predation rate may be more than double Fish and Wildlife Service estimate. The study, conducted in South Carolina, found that less than half the cats ate their prey and only 25% of the animals killed were brought home—the basis for how the first estimate was determined. Further, reptiles such as lizards were common prey—something that hadn't been documented in the past.

If you are a cat owner, you can help resolve this issue by making your cat an indoor cat (incidentally, it has been shown that bells on collars do not reduce predation by cats). It is a sure thing that indoor cats will not kill critters they are not supposed to. To find out how to make your cat an indoor cat, check out the American Bird Conservation website: http://www.abcbirds.org/cats/ and follow the two links under Background Information.

My original column notes on this subject started out as a diatribe against cats in general. Now, I find myself as part of the problem and with a view somewhat more understanding if not moderated. I plan to make my cat an indoor pet. Hopefully, you will do the same with your cat.

Coots

There was a recent news story about an 84 year-old woman arrested for repeatedly calling 911 because a pizza joint refused to deliver a single slice of pizza to her apartment. She wanted her pizza and, she wanted the person at the pizza place who called her "a crazy old coot" arrested.

Here we go again, slamming wildlife to describe aberrant human behavior. The American coot, *Fulica americana,* is not crazy nor does it deserve to be slandered because of geriatric humans who misbehave.

Coots are also known as mudhens, whitebills or splatterers. They are common marsh birds and are often mistaken for ducks. However, these black swimming birds with white beaks and red eyes are related to rails, not ducks. Their feet are not webbed and their triangular bills are not flattened like a duck's bill.

Coot chicks have been called adorable, but really, homely is generous. They are gray and yellow but the down looks prickly, not soft like a duckling. Their heads are initially bald with a black band encircling head and eyes like Zorro's mask.

If you have ever even driven past any type of marsh habitat in the warmer months, you have probably seen coots and likely lots of them. They are very common coast to coast and from northern Canada to South America.

However, unless you have stopped to actually watch coots, you have probably missed the show. While coots are not crazy, they do have charming antics that are fun to watch.

Coots seem to be constantly swimming, sometimes with their young on their back, using the wide lobes on their toes to good effect. Periodically they dive beneath the surface to reappear about 30 seconds later somewhere else. Bobbing their heads like pigeons, it seems that they have a constant chatter going with themselves.

Watching coots take flight is much like watching your kid wobble off on his or her maiden bicycle voyage. You want to run along and help them out. Because coots are configured to dive, with feet set far back on the body, take-off is a laborious process with the coot running along the water, wings flapping furiously, until the round body can get airborne.

One of the coot's most interesting behaviors was revealed by some recent research reported by National Geographic. Coots are nest parasites, meaning that they will lay eggs in other birds' nests in hopes of increasing the survival of their chicks. Coots parasitize other coots. That in itself is not so earth shattering. However, since they are all onto the game, it becomes important for a coot to be able to recognize its own eggs.

The research indicates that, indeed, coots can tell their own eggs from that of an entrepreneurial hen and may bury the eggs that don't belong. However, the most interesting part is that after a four year study, the authors are convinced that the coots can count! Hens that don't recognize parasitic eggs stop laying when the clutch reaches a certain size (thus reducing her own egg production). Hens that reject the imposters continue to lay eggs until the optimal clutch size is reached.

So, if brash youngsters ever call you an old coot, just wink and grin— coots are smarter than they think.

Read the article at:

http://news.nationalgeographic.com/news/2003/04/0402_030402_coots.html

Wooly Bear Weather Forecasters

In anticipation of writing of wooly bear caterpillars, I have been scouring the roads for the past several weeks looking for one inching its way across the pavement. I have seen snakes, dead cats and even a weasel, but the object of my search has eluded me. I had hoped to add a little realism but I suppose I can wing it from past experience.

The wooly bear caterpillar is famed for its skills as a meteorologist. It is not that the wooly bear makes jokes with the anchorman while pointing out the latest satellite image. It is much more subtle than that. It goes something like this, "Wide brown stripes on woolly bear caterpillars in the fall indicate a mild winter. But, if the brown stripe is narrow, prepare for a nasty long winter."

However, before I proceed with the weather-forecasting abilities of this humble insect-to-be, perhaps a brief description is in order. The wooly bear caterpillar is the larvae of the tiger moth, of which there are several hundred species in the United States. However, the common species picked for "weather forecasting" is specifically of the tiger moth, *Isia isabella*. Apparently, not just any tiger moth caterpillar will do.

The wooly bear caterpillar gets its name from its black/brown/black coloration of stiff bristles that resemble hairs and gives it a "wooly" appearance. It can be just over two inches long when fully developed.

The wooly bear has two other distinctions that are as interesting as any possible weather forecasting ability. The first is the fact that the wooly bear seeks shelter in the fall and hibernates through the winter—very rare among caterpillars. In the spring it emerges from hiding, eats, and then makes a cocoon from the stiff bristles of its shed skin.

The second fascinating thing about wooly bears is that when they are infested with parasitic fly larvae, they will seek out and consume poison hemlock. Apparently the wooly bear is better able to detoxify the poison than are the uninvited guests.

Back to meteorology. Jack Focht, director of Friends of the Woolly Bear, claims that the wooly bear has accurately predicted the weather 80 percent of the time since they began recording in 1946. However, research conducted by the American Museum of Natural History long ago concluded that the toss of a coin was as accurate at predicting the coming winter severity as the wooly bear. To wooly bear aficionados, that statement edges dangerously toward the biological equivalent of heresy.

However, current scientific research indicates that the width of the brown stripe is a function of how near the caterpillar is to maturity—the older the caterpillar, the wider the stripe. Hence, if you only measured fully mature caterpillars, the prediction would always be for a mild winter.

But, what the heck, bottom line is, if you want to believe in wooly bears as weather predictors, go right ahead. Given that the weatherman who makes the small talk with the anchorman is only right in his predictions 60 percent of the time, believing an insect makes about as much sense.

Nature's Historians

Last fall, on a campout adventure with a group of Boy Scouts, we spent the better part of a morning exploring several sink holes, with thirty-foot diameter round openings about ground level. Once we descended, there were several side channels, subterranean enough for a thrill when investigated by twelve and thirteen year olds with hyperactive imaginations, but safe enough that their leaders would actually follow them. Discoveries were fancifully examined as they were handed from boy to boy. Each jagged rock metamorphosed into an Indian artifact and each piece of bone into a prehistoric wonder. My fascination, though, was best captured by the middens that supplied many of these jewels—the treasure troves built by the bushy-tailed woodrats, true keepers of the history of the land.

Bushy-tailed woodrats (*Neotoma cinerea*) are the only woodrat common to our area. They are members of the Cricetidae family and count as second cousins voles, deer mice, lemmings and muskrats.

Bushy-tailed woodrats (and all other woodrats) proudly carry another moniker: packrats. This comes from their kleptomaniacal behavior of making off with virtually anything they can carry. These treasures include pinecones, sticks, bones, bits of rock and especially anything shiny or colorful. This habit can be disconcerting to untidy campers who may wake to find any number of small items missing from camp.

They stash their filched treasures in big piles that archaeologists call middens. These "garbage piles" seem to serve no purpose in furthering the success of individual woodrats or woodrat populations. Middens are stuffed with items that even a woodrat must find useless, yet they dedicate a tremendous amount of energy gathering it. But nature always seems to have a plan and energy is seldom frivolously wasted. This seemingly nonsensical neurotic shoplifter behavior has proven to be invaluable in unraveling the ecological mysteries of the past 50,000 years.

A woodrat gathers up its precious trophies from a territory that never exceeds a 100-meter diameter. As it adds each treasure to the pile, it also excretes a highly concentrated urine on the midden to mark it's territory. Over time, as this urine crystallizes, it becomes what paleoecologists (scientists who study pre-historic ecological relationships) call "amberat". It serves a similar function to the "amber" in which mosquitoes were trapped in the movie *Jurassic Park*, mummifying and gluing together everything in the midden. If the midden is protected from moisture, the crystallized urine can safeguard, apparently indefinitely and in a perfect state, all of the items that the packrats have stashed there.

Paleoecologists, using a technique called radiocarbon dating, can determine the age of a midden. Some middens have been found to be older than the 50,000-year limit of this technique. The scientists painstakingly inventory all the contents of the midden. Items may include sticks, seeds, fruits, leaves, insects and other invertebrates, lizard scales, and bones from any number of creatures. This information has become the richest and best-documented source of plant remains in the world.

Once multiple middens are dated for an area, the information is catalogued, and paleoecologists set about to reconstruct the vegetation and climate of a given era and place. One of the most important transitions they have examined occurred about 10,000 to 12,000 years ago as the continent entered into the current interglacial period at the end of the ice age. As the continent has warmed, vegetation and the landscape changed dramatically.

For instance, the scientists have discovered that at the beginning of the current period, most of what is now a desert was once a pinyon-juniper forest. Only those areas that currently receive about four inches of precipitation a year sustained true desert vegetation 10,000 years ago. By virtue of what was not there, middens also revealed that Ponderosa pine, a valuable tree common from Mexico to Canada, was absent in the landscape 10,000 years ago. Populations of this species may have arrived only in the last one or two millennia.

I feel a special kinship with the bushy-tailed woodrat. I squirrel away all manner of likely useless junk: bits and pieces of metal, various nuts, bolts and other hardware (enough to stock a modest store), and trinkets that time has proven I will never use. Like my grandfather before me who collected and kept literally everything, and at least one of my sons, I too am a packrat—only as a human, I dignify my quirkiness by calling myself a collector.

What is Your Batting Average?

If ever there were a creature in desperate need of an image consultant, it would have to be the bat. Even though bats are an extremely diverse group, they are usually lumped together and routinely maligned as creepy, blind, blood-sucking, hair tangling, rabies infested, dirty little flying rodents that associate with witches and vampires. All these accusations are totally false.

Each spring, 12 species of endemic Idaho bats emerge from hibernation and command our night skies. Two other species will return from warmer climes to join them as the only mammals to ever develop true flight.

Bats are members of the Order Chiroptera and have about 925 species (about 20 percent of all mammals are bats). Evolutionarily speaking, they are not even closely related to rodents. Scientists believe that they are more closely linked to primates (monkeys, humans etc.) than to rodents.

A bat's most unique adaptation, flight, may make it difficult not to think of a bat as a bird. However, bats are very different (so, why do I often instinctively reach first for my bird field guide when I want to identify a bat?). Their wings are living membranes stretched between their four fingers and body. Their forelimb structure is much like that of humans except the bones (particularly in their "hands") are greatly elongated. Their flight is incredibly agile and they are truly the aerobatic masters of the sky.

Bats are often divided into two major groups, usually given the rank of suborders: Megachiroptera and Microchiroptera. While this really doesn't have anything to do with size as the prefixes might imply, the smallest bat is a microchiropteran and weighs less than a penny. The largest bat happens to be a megachiropteran with a 40 inch wingspan and weighs three pounds.

Microchiropteran bats join a small group of animals that use echolocation for navigation. They emit ultrasonic waves with their larynx to locate solid objects as small as a human hair. This adaptation allows them to fly in total darkness. Echolocation is a short-range tool, though, and it is still miraculous how bats can consistently find their way back to their exact roosting spot after wandering for hours in the black of night.

Although many bats depend upon echolocation to navigate, bats are not blind. Megachiropterans, found only in the tropics, have large eyes with far better vision than humans and they do not echolocate. There is at least one species in the U.S. that is reported to have vision equaling military night vision optics.

Rabies is a common concern when people think of bats. However, they are no more prone to the disease than other wild mammals and do not "carry" the disease with immunity. The few people infected with rabies each year by bats likely contract the disease when they handle bats that are sick and acting strangely (such as allowing themselves to be picked up). This is a foolish practice with any animal.

There is a skeleton in the bat closet though, that tends to give all bats a bad rap. It seems that everyone has heard of the vampire bats of Central and South America. These only amount to three species, two of which only drink the blood of birds. Vampire bats don't actually suck blood like Dracula; rather, they make small incisions in their host and lap up the oozing blood.

Still a bit squeamish about bats? Here is one more thought: If there is one thing about bats that should give us nightmares, it is the possibility of a world without them.

Bats Are Essential

I ended the previous page about bats with the cryptic statement that if we are to fear something about bats, it should be a world without them. As chilling as that may sound, it may be a tremendous understatement.

Aside from the vampire bat, have you ever wondered what bats eat? Well, in North America, nearly every bat species is an insect eater. A single bat may eat several thousand insects a night. That is no small thing when you consider that a colony of 20 million free-tailed bats from Bracken Cave in central Texas, eat more than 200 tons of insects in a single mid-summer night. This fact alone is likely worth billions of dollars in insect control.

In tropical areas, there are also fruit bats and nectar-feeding bats. These bats are so important to the ecosystems they are sometimes referred to as "keystone species." Simply put, without them, the ecosystem would fall apart because the plants have co-evolved with the bats.

There are at least 300 species of plants, including food, medicinal and wood fiber plants in the Old World tropics alone, which are dependent on the seed dispersal and pollination abilities of bats. For example, over 95% of tropical reforestation of cleared land occurs because of the seed dispersal ability of bats.

Even though bats are critical components of most ecosystems, their numbers have been plummeting. Of the 44 species of bats in North America, over half are endangered or being considered for endangered species listing. This can happen very fast; in a ten year period, bats in Eagle Creek Cave in Arizona, formerly home to the world's largest bat colony, dropped from between 25 and 50 million to 30,000.

As is usually the case, there is no single culprit to blame for declining populations. Habitat destruction, poisoning with insecticides and deliberate annihilation have taken their toll. Disturbing wintering colonies in their hibernacula may also have devastating impacts. Each unnecessary intrusion can burn off as much as 30 days' worth of fat reserves when the bat has to rouse from hibernation to flee the commotion. Repeated disruption can quickly eliminate a colony. And now, there is another storm rising: white-nose syndrome. This infectious fungal disease from the Old World is devastating bat colonies. It started in the East and has been moving inexorably westward.

So, with all that said, what should you do if you have a bat in your belfry (attic)? Despite their importance, it is still not a good practice to allow bats and humans to occupy the same dwelling, so practicality says the bat must go. However, you can soften the blow by first installing a bat house (see websites below) to give the bats an alternate home (keeping them around can help control garden pests). Then, identify and block off the entrances to the dwelling after you are sure all the bats have left for the night. It is best to do this before the females have pups or after the pups can leave on their own.

Bats are wonderful creatures worthy of our awe, admiration, and thanks. They have done far more to save the world than Batman ever thought of doing.

Information:
To learn more about bats and bat conservation, how to build a bat house or where to buy a bat house, check out the following websites: http://www.batcon.org/ www.wildbirdsforever.com .

Metamorphosis

The huge ungainly caterpillar on a backyard plant made me laugh. It wasn't cute like a wooly bear caterpillar, nor was it fascinating like the caterpillar of a sphinx moth. Its brownish body was fatter than a pencil, nearly two inches long and had large pale eyespots on a humped-up fore end. More faint spots stretched down each side, but in a word, it was kind of ugly. I called my wife over for a look. She leaned in closely, grimaced, and asked, "What is it?" I didn't know. Was it harmful, beneficial or benign? I didn't know that either.

Later, I checked my field guide and determined that it was the caterpillar of one of the swallowtail family of butterflies, probably the Western swallowtail. No way. That homely caterpillar would become one of the most beautiful of butterflies? It hardly seemed possible.
Without trusting in a guidebook, there was not a single thing about that caterpillar that would lead anyone to believe that it would become a flying flower. It had no wings, no antennae, not even real-looking legs. If it weren't for the eyespots, calling it homely would be generous.

It wasn't even the right color. Swallowtail butterflies are either a colorful swirl of black and yellow or black and white. Their caterpillars are green or striped, not brown. Cathy surfed the internet, though, and found an apology for the plainness of our caterpillar. A brown swallowtail caterpillar is one that is nearing pupation.

When I returned outside several hours later with my camera, I could still see the stickiness the caterpillar had left of the leaf, but it was gone. Maybe one of the dozens of robins in the yard had made a deluxe meal of it. I was excited to think that my backyard could produce swallowtails so I preferred to imagine that it crawled to a safe place and was now secure inside it's chrysalis.

It is pretty easy to understand the biology of a caterpillar. It is an eating machine, rapidly growing and molting in preparation for becoming an adult. The biology of an adult is also relatively straightforward: stay alive, pollinate a few flowers while feeding, find a mate and reproduce.

But, getting from a caterpillar, homely or otherwise, into a swallowtail butterfly is the messy part. Science explains it in one word: metamorphosis, as if this answers everything in a process yet to be understood. If there is true magic in nature, metamorphosis is surely a candidate.

Inside that chrysalis, wonderful and unexplainable things happen. The body of the caterpillar disintegrates and a new and completely different one is formed from the spare parts. It is like melting a rubber life raft and, without adding any parts, re-assembling it into a Ferrari. Oh, except that the raft would have to do the work itself. While it sleeps. And it works every time; neither the caterpillar nor the butterfly need think about it.

Metamorphosis isn't so easy for us humans. Despite opposable thumbs and huge brains, it has been said that most of us go to our graves with our music still in us. There is a beautiful butterfly in each of us, but releasing it may be life's greatest struggle.

Snakes Alive!

A cardinal rule in snake country is to never show your fear. Unlike with vicious dogs or African lions, this has nothing to do with the snake sensing your terror and moving in for the kill. In the case of rattlers, it is to protect you from the debased sense of humor of your companions who may go to great lengths to prey upon your weakness once they discover it.

My friend Jon is a perfect example. Jon made the monumental mistake of openly admitting his distaste and fear of snakes and has become a marked man. For a planned float trip down the Salmon River, a locale well known for "buzztails," two malicious companions realized the wicked opportunity the trip presented. They dispatched a hapless large rattler before the trip, carefully coiled it and froze it into position. Then it was discreetly wrapped and placed in the cooler with the food and loaded onto the raft.

The timing for the prank was ripe after a day afloat where they saw several rattlers on the beaches and spent the evening telling scary snake stories around the fire. When Jon's tolerance for the stories reached its limit, he carefully moved off to bed. Preparing to climb into bed, he threw back his sleeping bag and saw the coiled snake, subsequently setting a new unofficial record for the high jump. Mark and Tony, of course, nearly went apoplectic with glee.

It seems, though, regardless of where a person's sentiments lie in regard to snakes, everyone has a snake story. Some are routine, others hilarious and a few are enough to send icy fingers down your spine.

My grandmother loved to tell the story of how she bravely beat a rattler to a pulp with a shovel. Then she proudly laid the poor thing on the porch and went to find her father. But when she returned, the snake was gone, never to be seen again.

When my son, Jacob, was about thirteen, we bumped into a large rattlesnake on a family outing. Jacob really wanted this trophy and I agreed to let him kill it provided he tanned the skin, ate the flesh and put the head in a jar of alcohol (for educational purposes). In keeping his end of the bargain, he was straightening the fangs out and propping the mouth open to make a proper demonstration piece as I had instructed him, while at the same time trying to keep his brother out of the house. With characteristic zeal, brother Ben charged the door which hit Jake so hard he lost his grip on the snake head. Just like Murphy's law that states that the toast always lands buttered side down, this snake's head, fangs carefully propped into striking position, bounced onto Jake's arm and hung there, one fang penetrating the skin. Against my advice, Cathy insisted on taking him to the emergency room, "just in case," but the story doesn't end there. Cathy is a registered nurse. She was at a hospital staff meeting months later when the director of nursing mentioned the incident under the, "you wouldn't believe how stupid people can be" part of his talk!

We still have that snake head in a jar and it serves to remind me that behind the fierce, unblinking, frightening eyes of a rattlesnake, masked by that heart- stopping warning buzz, is an animal with a wicked sense of humor.

Chipmunks

With apparent ease, the chipmunk raced, tail straight up, across the log I was standing on, under another, and part way up a tree. It disappeared around the trunk momentarily, but scampered back into view within seconds. For a moment or two, it would sit back on its haunches and examine a bit of potential food or, I assumed, look out for predators; then it was off again on its energetic and unpredictable way. The brief encounter brought a smile and instant success to an otherwise fruitless hunt.

Chipmunks are, in my opinion, the cutest and most entertaining animals in the woods—and one of the most easily recognizable. In fact, I doubt if there is an animal less likely to need a description than a chipmunk. I cannot conceive of anyone over ten years old who has not seen many chipmunks in their life.

Although there are 15 species of chipmunks in the west, at first glance they all share enough characteristics to be instantly recognizable as a group. Chipmunks are small, with bodies four to six inches long and weighing just a few ounces. All have facial stripes (black through the eye bordered by white stripes), and black, white and/or brown stripes along the back with a tan or brown body. Their frenetic activity, as they dash about gathering food or chasing one another, is another giveaway clue. They have to be the most active animal in the woods and fields.

In the west, the least chipmunk is the most widely distributed, occurring from the Dakotas to California and Southern Canada to Mexico. As the name implies, it is the smallest of the chipmunks. It is distinguished by its small size, dorsal stripes that run all the way to the base of the tail, small ears and a tail that points straight up when it runs. It can also be found in a wide variety of habitats from open pine forests to desert badlands.

Although chipmunks hibernate the winter away, they are quite different from ground squirrels. A ground squirrel stores its winter food in the form of fat and does not stir from hibernation until spring. A chipmunk, on the other hand, stores the food itself and wakes periodically to eat. If the food supply runs out before the winter ends, the chipmunk may starve to death.

So, all that frenetic, crazed chasing about is an effort to gather enough food to last through the winter. They use the daylight hours to gather seeds, fruits, fungi, flowers and just about anything else that is edible, including insects, eggs and young vertebrates.

It is a sad commentary that we tend to judge everything in nature against the yardstick of utility to humanity. Some would argue that a chipmunk isn't much good if it isn't a target or directly useful in some other way. They fail to understand the ecological role chipmunks play as seed dispersers and prey for a large number of hungry predators.

But if chipmunks are to be judged with this litmus test, I hope you will reach the same verdict that I have—their value for elk hunts salvaged, smiles and laughs rendered, and spirits lifted is incalculable.

Skunks

It was enough to strike terror in my heart. There were my little kids, playing in the neighbor's yard. Innocent enough, I suppose, until one of them came running back to get me and show me what they were playing with. Four baby skunks! Like in the movie, *The Exorcist*, my head spun a complete 360 degree circle. My eyes scanned the edges of the bushes like twin periscopes looking for a black and white torpedo streaking our way, ready to gas us and then gnaw our legs off while we choked.

There are few animals, the mere presence of which, humans really don't tolerate very well. Usually it is because we fear them. Rattlesnakes, scorpions, spiders, and skunks all come to mind. Inoffensive creatures in their own right, but they do have the ability to make us miserable should we trespass against them.

The striped skunk, *Mephitis mephitis*, is one of four skunks native to the United States; including one other one that my field guide indicates also inhabits Idaho. However, I have never seen a spotted skunk, dead or alive, in eastern Idaho. The striped skunk, though, is common throughout the United States, southern Canada and northern Mexico.

If there ever was a mammal that did not need a description, it is likely the striped skunk. Who can't close their eyes and easily visualize the following: a body roughly the size of a house cat closely followed by a bushy tail about 7-10 inches long. Color, no—black and white. The body is black and a white stripe begins on the forehead and runs to the tail. About the front shoulders, the stripe splits into two parallel lines. The pattern is highly variable, though.

It isn't their looks that make skunks scary. Skunks stink. They can readily defend themselves and they know it. More, they can transfer that potent stink to any creature foolish enough to aggravate them. The transfer occurs when the skunk aims head and rear at the transgressor, raises its tail, arches its back, and fires two streams of musk from glands just inside the anus. They are reported to be accurate to 10 feet but I am confident that a near miss would still send me gagging. And don't be fooled, if they miss, there is still enough juice for five to six more tries.

True omnivores, skunks feed on just about anything, including insects, vegetation, eggs, small birds and mammals and carrion. Occasionally they cause a problem in chicken coops but most often their eating habits are beneficial to man.

Skunks are mainly nocturnal and here their black coat serves them well. The contrasting white stripe (anti-camouflage) also serves a purpose as it lets would be predators know with what they will be tangling. Predators including foxes and coyotes may occasionally eat a skunk but great horned owls that can swoop in on silent wings are by far the most effective predators.

Skunks are habitat generalists and can be found just about anywhere, but are generally found within several miles of water. Since they are mostly nocturnal, you are most likely see them after dark, preferably in your headlights and preferably before they go *thunk* under your tires.

I don't recommend getting up close and personal with a skunk like my kids did. Not only do they smell terrible, (I can always tell when one has passed through my yard) they can make you smell terrible. Worse, they can bite you and skunks are one of the leading hosts for rabies. Admire and fear them from a distance.

What to do if you are sprayed by a skunk:

If you get sprayed by a skunk, be prepared for some discomfort. The smell is nauseating and can cause nasal passages to swell and eyes to water. A direct hit into the eyes can cause a temporary blinding sensation but it is not permanent.

The following recipe (developed by a chemist) is effective in removing skunk odor: In an OPEN container, combine 1 quart fresh **hydrogen peroxide**, 0.25 cup of baking soda, and 1 or 2 teaspoons of liquid dish soap or laundry detergent. Apply liberally. Don't try to store any extra as the hydrogen peroxide and baking soda make a potent mix (hence the OPEN container).

Drakes in Drag—Eclipse Plumage

Down on the Snake River Greenbelt in July, it looked like a disease had afflicted the mallard ducks. Female mallards were plentiful but males were few. Those drakes that were still present were strangely attired. The usually resplendent heads were mottled brown, some with patches of green iridescence splashed like spilled paint. Chests, backs, and bellies also showed a bizarre mix of coloration. What sort of evil was plaguing our ducks? Were they mutants, crossbreeds, or diseased? And where had the rest of the drakes gone?

In reality, none of the above was true. The males were still there, dressed in drag and hidden in plain sight. This is the season where the drakes of many species of ducks molt their breeding and flight feathers and for several weeks masquerade as hens while their flight feathers regenerate.

Although feathers are strong and durable, they eventually wear out and need replacing. In some birds, such as raptors, this replacement is a slow process, particularly with the flight feathers. Otherwise, a flightless eagle would starve before its feathers grew back.

With ducks the process is much faster and many feathers are replaced at once. Ducks like mallards cannot fly during this time and a brightly colored male would be an easy target for a predator.

Although wing color in the speculum doesn't change, the male replaces the rest of his brightly colored feathers with drab ones that strongly resemble the female and provide better camouflage. This is called the basic or eclipse plumage, and during this time, males can be difficult to differentiate from females.

For mallards, the easiest field technique for telling a male from a female during the summer months is to look at the bill. The male has a yellow to light green bill with a black spot at the tip. The female's bill is orange with lots of black on top.

The eclipse plumage doesn't last very long. Mallards begin courtship in the fall and must molt back into their breeding plumage by early autumn. This second molt doesn't include the wing feathers. Of course, this is a process and produces some comical-looking males as they progress from drag back to dress-up. Many will look like crossbreeds or no species in particular and may make identification confusing at times.

It is interesting to note that not all ducks have an eclipse plumage. The pintail drake, for example, does not change his plumage even though he still goes through a molt.

While eclipse plumage for the mallard is short-lived, other ducks may maintain the basic plumage much longer. Blue-winged teal and shoveler drakes may be found in their drab eclipse plumage well into winter.

As I watched the ducks on the Greenbelt, occasional squabbles made it obvious that even though it was more challenging for me to tell the males from the females, the ducks had no problem. The hens would tolerate the drakes in full breeding plumage but repeatedly chased off those in eclipse plumage. Just goes to show, it pays to look your best.

Dancing With Sharptails

Long ago, some friends invited my wife and I to go line dancing, a popular country dance style at the time. My wife really enjoys that sort of thing and so I tried to be a good sport for her sake. But after an evening of fruitless instruction, I added line dancing to a growing list of things I was just not cut out to do. I told my wife then that I thought dancing was for the birds and I meant it.

Over the years, I have introduced several friends to the true artists of dancing, the sharp-tailed grouse. In most of the West, that specifically means the subspecies *columbiana*, or the Columbian Sharp-tailed Grouse. The males of this species really know how to shake a leg and I have never had anyone walk away disappointed or unimpressed after seeing the show.

Like sage-grouse, sharp-tailed grouse gather in the spring on to traditional dancing grounds called leks. Here, each male carves out a territory and dances with gleeful abandon in an effort to attract females, intimidate rivals and, I think, just for the sheer joy of it.

The sharp-tailed grouse gets its name from the fact that the middle two feathers on the tail are about one inch longer than their counterparts. It seems a rather useless modification until you see them dance. Then the tail becomes a semaphore flag. It raises straight up into the air, revealing a brilliant white triangular-shaped underside. The two tallest feathers vibrate side to side in a blur sure to attract feminine attention.

While perhaps not as striking as the male sage-grouse, the male sharptail is still a handsome fellow. The natural coloration of the bird is a perfect camouflage of browns, blacks, grays, and tans. When displaying, his dance costume includes yellow "eyebrows" and purple air sacs on each side of his neck.

The sharp-tailed grouse dance is much more vigorous and synchronized than that of the stately sage-grouse. Males arrive well before dawn, and for the next several hours wear themselves out displaying and chasing each other. The dance begins when the bird extends head and neck, raises his tail to the sky, and holds his wings out parallel to the ground. Then as he circles about, he stomps his feet like he is trying to stamp out a bed of hot coals, and creates a sound like a drum roll. This apparently drives the lady grouse wild.

I tried this with a class of 2nd graders once: I had all the boys stand up, bend at the waist, extend their arms and stomp their feet while moving in a circle. All the girls thought it was funny, but I didn't get any indication they were impressed.

What still amazes me is that the lek can be completely still, with all pairs of males hunkered down, facing each other, and mutually chastising each other with a series of clucks and coos. Without any signal that I can detect, all the birds on the lek (my favorite lek usually has about 25 males) jump up and simultaneously begin to dance, filling the air with a sound like heavy rain falling on a roof. Tails flash in the sun, birds chase each other, fly short distances, and then, as suddenly as it begins, it is over and they are back into hunkering mode. This on again off again dancing may last until about 9:00 a.m. when they fly from the lek to gather enough food to give them the energy to be able to do it again in the morning.

When my wife gets the urge to do a little dancing, I fully intend to remind her that just as we leave the driving to Greyhound and fried chicken to the Colonel, I choose to leave dancing to the birds, specifically the all natural, all native sharp-tailed grouse.

Crane Flies

The young lady was worried. She had just escaped from the largest mosquito she had ever seen and it was still lurking outside her door. She described it as Texas-sized, having a body nearly an inch long with six absurdly long legs spreading almost two inches at rest. Indeed, a terrifying mosquito—if it had been one.

Even when I explained that the insect she saw was only a harmless crane fly, the young lady was skeptical and refused to leave her house.

Crane flies are huge, no doubt about it. The giant crane fly of the Pacific Northwest may have a wingspan of three inches and a tip to tip leg spread nearly double that. They are part of the Order Diptera which does include the mosquitoes and also other familiar insects such as house flies, deer flies and horseflies. Unlike some of its irritating relatives, the adult crane fly is harmless; most species don't even possess mouth parts with which to feed.

Like all dipterans, the crane fly undergoes a complete metamorphosis from a larval stage to adult stage. Among the nearly 300 species of crane flies, this change from grub to flying insect may take from several months up to five years.

During the larval stage, crane flies perform a great service for the ecosystem. The larvae grow fat by eating decaying material and helping the decomposition process that reduces waste and recycles nutrients. Depending on the species, crane fly larvae can be found from stream beds to deserts. The majority inhabit moist soils and litter layers and many are aquatic, providing a secondary benefit as food for a variety of fish.

There are a few exotic or, non-native, species of crane flies that can cause damage to lawns when in the larval stage. They will burrow through the lawn eating the roots. Turning the sod of sick-looking lawn may reveal large brownish larvae.

Adult crane flies may only live a week or two. Their primary purpose is to find another crane fly of the opposite sex and mate. Females then deposit eggs in the ground or water. With this all important event out of the way, the adults die.

About the only irritation caused by adult crane flies is the fact that they are attracted to white light and may gather in unacceptable numbers on porches. Then when the door opens, a few slip inside. Other than having insects in the house, they really do no harm: with no mouthparts, they cannot bite us or damage our property, if they don't eat they don't poop; and they are not attracted to nasty things outside so they are not likely to be vectors of disease. Try a yellow colored bulb if crane fly congregations are a problem on your porch.

Last week as I entered my office door, I paused to watch a young praying mantis put the stalk on a crane fly. When I bent closer for a better view, my movement startled the fly and it took flight. I felt guilty ruining the mantis' day, but enjoyed knowing that the crane fly might live long enough to find a mate and fulfill its destiny.

Marks of Autumn

Vehicles lined the road on both sides, a telltale sign in Yellowstone National Park that an animal had been spotted. But what was it? I have seen traffic jams like this for a lowly coyote, but I was hoping for elk. The sapling-sized trees, re-growth after the fires of 1988, made a visually impenetrable screen though, and despite our rubbernecking, we could see nothing.

Then I saw the top of a single sapling, perhaps twelve feet tall, shake back and forth like it had been grabbed by the Devil himself. We stopped in the middle of the road and I jumped out, camera in hand; for this was a sure sign that a bull elk or moose was torturing that hapless sapling to death with its antlers.

It was a bull elk, six massive antler points per side, and he was showing no mercy to that tree. He raked his antlers up and down, hooking and gouging the four-inch trunk. A twist of his rut-swollen neck and the sapling bent nearly in half. Sap oozed from a skinned trunk section two feet long. Branches and strips of bark flew as he methodically attacked the tree for about ten minutes.

The sapling's beating was a reminder that the rut had begun, and from August to November, almost no tree or shrub is safe from an attack by a testosterone-crazed, antler-wearing male of the deer family. Any species of tree is in danger so long as it is alive. Saplings are preferred, although I have seen elk thrash trees far larger.

Once a tree has been abused by a bull or a buck, it is called a rub. At first their purpose is clear: to help remove the velvet that has nourished the growing antler bone all summer long. Once the velvet is rubbed free though, males continue to rake trees, often scraping a dozen or more in a small area. They are marking territories and advertising to the ladies to be sure, but I suspect many rubs are just a way to release hormone induced frustration.

A few clues will often tell you which species made the rub. Bucks tend to choose smaller trees than elk or moose and rub the tree closer to the ground. An elk or moose rub may be three or four feet off the ground, sometimes higher. Occasionally, the damage may be significantly higher if the bull has bent the tree toward the ground and then raked upward, and they also sometimes break off the tops. Hairs may become stuck in the sap of the tree and can identify the attacker—elk hair is long and brown, mule deer is gray and moose is black. Scent can also give it away. An elk rub scented in urine is unmistakable.

This past week there have been many signs that autumn is here: a skiff of snow in Yellowstone, crisp cool days, a few trees already in autumn color, a frosted garden. None of these, though, says autumn like finding a tree freshly brutalized by an elk, moose, or deer scraping velvet and polishing bone to an ivory hue.

Flying in a Flock

The snow buntings fed along the roadside edge. Each time a car passed they sprang into the air simultaneously. They would turn, tuck, and dive like a single organism. First left, then as if charged by electrical current, they pivoted right, up then down, in perfect coordination. There were no collisions, no misguided ones that went, F-Troop style, contrary to the flock. They seemed to act as one collective mind. They were doing what seemed impossible: coordinating hundreds of bodies in unplanned, unpracticed, random movement 3-D flight and, to my eye, doing it perfectly.

Avian flight in any form is delightful, but when some flocks gather, even ordinary birds become far more than the sum of their individual effort. Like a caterpillar becoming a butterfly, flock flight metamorphoses into a mystical aerial ballet. It is straight from the sorcerer's wand and understood by humans at only the most rudimentary levels.

Like a garnish on your favorite dish, what little is known about flock behavior tends to make it more interesting, even more mysterious. Most flock behavior is linked to avoiding predators. With so many eyes, there is always someone looking in every direction. In flight, predators tend to avoid the flock, possibly concerned about injury or confused by the mass, so flock behavior makes ecological sense.

High speed photography reveals that there is not likely a single leader in a flock. Following a few rules, any member of the flock can initiate a movement, but not all movement initiates the wave. For example, a bird that turns away from the flock will likely be ignored as such a move increases the risk of predation.

Each movement of the flock begins with an individual's movement. Members within its sphere of influence react to that movement and like a shock wave, it moves throughout the entire flock. The surge is incredibly fast, moving from bird to bird far faster than the normal reaction time would allow. In what has come to be known as the chorus line hypothesis (after the Music City Rockettes dancers), birds respond in one third their normal reaction time because they watch what is going on around them and anticipate their reaction.

The chorus line hypothesis hiccup is that it pre-supposes that the bird is able to be cognizant of everything around it. Flock flying is three dimensional where the movement wave may come from any direction, including above, below, or behind. How does a bird keep track of it all? What if dozens of birds in the flock all react to different stimuli at the exact same time, creating multiple movement waves? Wouldn't that lead to chaos, flock meltdown?

When we watch a flock of a million or more starlings flash and undulate through the air, collapsing then expanding like a bellows, doubling back, swooping low like living smoke on an enchanted breeze, it is obvious that these are not problems for the birds, only for the researchers.

My appreciation for the marvels of the aerial ballets performed every day in our skies probably wouldn't diminish if the mysteries of flock flying were completely solved. But on the other hand, I do enjoy knowing that there are secrets Nature still clutches tightly, and maybe, just maybe, we will never figure them all out.

Resource: to watch a fascinating 5 minute video of huge flocks of starlings at Ot Moor near Oxford, England, check out:
http://www.youtube.com/watch?v=XH-groCeKbE

Just a Robin?

An American robin flew from an aspen along a seldom used sidewalk as I approached. She scolded me as she left and I was immediately suspicious. Sure enough, when I peeked into the aspen, a nest was cradled in a branch fork. The cup-shaped nest was made of twigs and grass (I once found one in a juniper tree that was made mainly from strands of a blue tarp) and inside were four newly hatched robin chicks.

The American robin (*Turdus migratorius*) is just that, a bird of the Americas, breeding throughout Canada and the United States and wintering as far south as Guatemala. The Disney film *Mary Poppins*, which is set in London, UK, incorrectly portrays American robins singing by a window instead of the unrelated smaller European robin. Hollywood thinks we don't notice, but we do.

It is almost a sure thing that when an American robin visits your yard, the bird book can stay in the drawer. They have got to be one of the easiest birds on the planet to recognize. Their red breast, situated beneath a brown back, is the prose of story and song. Under the tail feathers is a large spot of white and there is a white crescent over each eye. Males are about ten inches long, somewhat larger and brighter colored than females. Immature robins have spots on paler orange breast feathers.

American robins love open grasslands with interspersed trees and shrubs, making backyard habitats ideal for them. In fact, they are one of several species of wildlife that has adapted well to humanity, and so long as we give them a little room, they will likely continue to do so.

Although robins are omnivorous, they aren't excited by the average seed filled bird feeder. Insects and berries are more their style. They excel at controlling many garden pests including larvae of all sorts, grasshoppers, beetles, nematodes, and worms. During brood rearing, I have watched the male robin make dozens of trips to the nest, each time with a bill filled like a grocery bag with all manner of crawling, jumping and flying critters.

Sixty percent of their diet is berries. Some of the berry bushes you can plant in your yard to attract American robins include: mountain or European ash, sand cherry, serviceberry, currants, and chokecherry. My half dozen chokecherry bushes often never even have the chance to ripen before robins clean them out. As a bonus, having a preferred food like chokecherries also reduces their interest in my strawberries and raspberries.

Spring seems to arrive on robin wings. Males get here first and a lively competition ensues as they establish territories. As the females begin to show up, still mornings are filled with song as the males sing like opera stars trying to woo a female to their territory. They mate for the season and may produce two clutches of powder blue eggs from April to July. The female builds a new nest for each clutch and does almost all of the incubation.

The American Robin has always been a popular bird: Crayola has a crayon color, robin's egg blue; it has been on Canada's $2 note; and the robin is the official state bird of Connecticut, Michigan, and Wisconsin.

Because they are so common, we may take American robins for granted, forgetting to enjoy and appreciate their presence. After all, they are only robins, right?

Colony Nesting

After driving around in Seattle's traffic during Memorial Day weekend and wading through mobs of noisy, jostling humanity, I was thrilled to return to the relatively uncrowded lifestyle of eastern Idaho. I can better appreciate having a little space around me.

A lot of wildlife feel the same way, seeking seclusion, especially during that vulnerable stage when eggs or young are still in the nest or helpless in the den. However, about one in eight bird species actually seeks out its own kind to nest in crowded, boisterous, noisy colonies. This is particularly true of what bird scientists refer to as waterbirds, or birds that make a living in, on or near the water, such as ibises, storks, cormorants, herons, egrets, puffins, shearwaters, gulls and terns.

Colonies, also called rookeries for some species, can vary in size from a few nests to almost a million nests crammed tightly together. In more crowded sites, each nest may be just out of pecking reach of the neighbors. Some of these sites are highly traditional. The same birds may return year after year and select the exact same nest location each time.

Colonies can occur from water's edge to the tops of the tallest trees. Grebes, some gulls, ibises, and terns may nest on floating vegetation, or muskrat houses, or build nests among the reeds. Other species prefer bare or sandy ground, rocky islands, or even cliffs. Still others, such as great blue herons, anhingas, and great egrets prefer to nest in trees.

Colony nesting adds a factor of safety and often the birds share communal duties that benefit the entire group, such as predator detection, defense, and parenting. More interesting, many colonies are communities with mixed species—with grebes, gulls, terns, ibises and more all nesting in close proximity and presumably adding to the security of all members of the colony. The rookery at Market Lake Wildlife Management Area is one such multi-species colony.

Rookeries and colonies are often in the best possible location available and that may account for extremely high numbers in some cases. It may be close to a food source, the most secure habitat in an altered landscape, or an island where mammalian predators are absent, such as the pelican nesting island in Blackfoot Reservoir.

Colonial nesting has another anti-predation advantage. Many colonial birds have synchronous breeding and subsequent hatching where almost all the chicks hatch at once. This effectively overwhelms the predators. Predators still get some, but the chicks quickly outgrow their vulnerable stage before predators can have an impact on the population.

Bird colonies also have the opposite effect, though. Colonies are often very noisy and, combined with the sheer mass of prey, may actually attract predators. In a bizarre case of learning and adaptation, normally fish-eating pelicans on the South African island, Malgas, have learned to hunt and swallow whole cape gannet chicks. This adapted predator is decimating colonies because the gannets have no evolved defense.

That is the other danger of a colonial breeding strategy: the colonies are very susceptible to disruption and disease, natural calamity, human interference, or in the case of the cape gannet, a new and mobile predator. One single event has the potential to devastate an entire colony.

Colony nesting birds have adapted to live together despite their differences. They have even found ways to derive mutual benefit from their associations. Humans could learn from that.

Insignificance

Over a fall weekend, I was in Yellowstone National Park, principally to photograph the rutting elk. However, the trip quickly turned into frustration and began to resemble my wildly unsuccessful attempts to hunt elk with a bow and arrow. I just seemed to be in the wrong place at the right time and vice versa.

On the second afternoon, I decided to drive the less traveled, dirt surfaced Blacktail Plateau road. As I entered a stand of Douglas fir trees, I noticed that the car about 100 yards ahead had stopped in the middle of the road. In the Park, this usually only happens when there is some wildlife to look at so I coasted to a stop. I could see a young buck mule deer feeding unconcernedly on the uphill side of the road.

I composed a few photos from the truck before I heard a car behind me and realized that I needed to move off the road so others could get by. I jockeyed the vehicle into a small wide spot in the road while keeping an eye on the deer. I must confess that at this point, I didn't have much faith in my luck. It had been my experience that Park animals further from the well traveled roads were much less accepting of humans. I assumed that the buck would either bolt or simply walk off faster than I could follow if I tried to close the distance.

Once the truck was re-positioned, though, I had nothing to lose in trying. I grabbed my gear and started up the hill. The buck seemed to ignore me but I wondered how he had gotten twenty yards to my right without my seeing him move. Then I realized there were two bucks, both almost identical in size. This epiphany had barely sunk in when I discerned a third buck, another yearling, this one with spike antlers, standing between his two larger companions.

I slowly moved up the steep slope, expecting with each step to have the bucks race off. The bucks were about 30 yards away and while they noticed me, they appeared unconcerned. I was careful to stay very visible at all times—just the opposite of hunting—and I really did not attempt to be quiet. I wanted them to know I was there, evaluate me as non-threatening and go about their business.

I watched them as they carefully selected the leaves of forbs and shrubs to eat, scratched at an ear with a hind foot, and even squatted for relief. I was so mesmerized by the scene playing out before me that I sometimes forgot the camera in my hand.

This went on for half an hour or so and then the nearest buck amazed me by repeatedly scraping the ground with his left hoof. He was preparing to bed down right in front of me! He sank to his knees and then his belly. Soon his twin did the same. Eventually, the spike scraped out a bed and lay down as well.

Although they seemed to ignore me, the bucks were otherwise ever watchful. Their huge ears worked like radar, constantly swiveling, often in opposite directions as they scanned for danger. It was clear that eternal vigilance was the key to survival in their world filled with lions, coyotes, wolves, and bears. Something out of sight to the east repeatedly caught their attention. Often, as a trio, they would turn to look in that direction, both ears swiveling forward for maximum detection capability.

During this period of relative inactivity, I did the only sensible thing—I joined them for a short nap. That was definitely a first for me, sharing nap time with three wild mule deer. I depended upon their vigilance to warn me of danger.

All in all, our encounter lasted about two hours. During that time, I began to speak to them, thanking them for their patience. At one point I even sang them a few John Denver tunes. I finally broke off our encounter with a wave. They did not wave back, but I didn't mind.

Even though I completed my Master of Science degree researching mule deer, I have never had such a unique opportunity. These deer appeared to behave as if I did not exist or was no more a curiosity than a squirrel or a jay. Never has insignificance felt so important!

Ticked Off

Most people just don't believe the kinds of things that I like to collect. For instance, I have a small vial on my desk full of wood ticks preserved in alcohol. These were the ticks that were brash enough to fasten themselves to me, my dog, and at least one, to my daughter. Some are just ticks; others are engorged blobs with tiny legs jutting straight out. All are long dead. I do get an unusual satisfaction from ending their blood-sucking careers.

Ticks are dreaded by most people. At work, all I have to do is just show a tick to a colleague of mine to turn him into a 6'2" hunk of jelly that runs down the hall screaming like a girl.

Ticks are not insects; they are more closely related to spiders and mites. They have eight legs and are generally flattened dorso-ventrally (back to stomach). There are about 800 species worldwide, giving tick haters plenty of targets.

The near-universal repulsiveness of ticks comes from the fact that they suck blood for a living. And they don't just do it with a quick bite like a mosquito. No, a tick buries its mouthparts into your flesh, cements itself on and, if undetected, dines for a period of several days. Few people like the thought of providing breakfast, lunch, and dinner for an unwanted guest, especially when the menu is blood. Our blood.

Rounding out their sinister reputation, ticks are one of the major vectors of the bacteria that cause maladies in humans such as Rocky Mountain Spotted Fever, Lyme Disease (this one comes from deer ticks which don't live in Idaho), and tularemia.

One of the most interesting illnesses, one that is known to affect people as well as dogs, is tick paralysis. The tick's saliva contains a neurotoxin which slowly causes paralysis in some cases. If a tick remains undetected for long enough, the toxin can begin to affect motor function, and in some cases causes death. Removal of the tick almost always initiates a quick and complete recovery. My wife, Cathy, actually saw a case like this as a nurse in northern Idaho.

Normally, ticks are just a part of life for all wild mammals and birds, but extreme cases of infestation are not unusual. I have seen moose covered with ticks and research has shown that an overburden of ticks can kill them. And just like with humans, ticks are also major transmitters of disease among animals.

Over the years, I have seen enough ticks that they don't have the psychological impact on me that they have on many people. It started years ago, when I accompanied my friend, a research biologist, as he checked out a dead elk. As we turned to leave, I was shocked to see that my friend's back was covered with ticks. With a shrug he admitted that it was pretty common in that area to end up with dozens of ticks when he checked a carcass. Hundreds of ticks would abandon the cooling body and crawl onto adjacent brush hoping for another meal to come by—in this case, my friend.

Spring and early summer are the tick season. After a trip to the field during that period, it is wise to check yourself over for ticks. If you find one already attached, remove it as soon as possible. As my economics professor used to say, there is no such thing as a free lunch—and that should apply to ticks too.

HOW TO SAFELY REMOVE A TICK
1. With a pair of tweezers, grasp the tick as close to the skin surface as possible. This reduces the possibility of the head separating from the rest of the body when being removed.
2. Pull the tick straight out with steady, even pressure. Do not twist or jerk because you may break the tick, leaving the mouthparts in the skin.
3. After removing the tick, thoroughly disinfect the bite site.

Do not apply Vaseline, a hot match, or grease to the rear of the tick. These actions can cause the tick to salivate while still in your skin, which can increase the likelihood of contracting a disease.

Bird Migration

Thanksgiving leftovers weren't even cold when we pointed our car south with the intention of driving as far as we could without passports. We would visit relatives, enjoy a brief respite from obstinate and early winter weather and, I hoped, have a chance to see some of our birds that had recently vacated Idaho for warmer weather where the southern corners of Arizona and California collide.

The roadsides at our destination were lined with hundreds of mourning doves and, I knew that 640 miles to the east of our planned route Idaho sandhill cranes were winging toward Bosque Del Apache National Wildlife Refuge south of Albuquerque, New Mexico.

Idaho birds are scattered across a broad winter landscape along the border with Mexico, to the Texas gulf coast, and deep into South America. We had a GPS to help us in our travels, but how birds navigate long distances, in some cases 10,000 miles apart, is still largely a mystery.

Migration is complex, but science is slowly beginning to unravel the unknowns. For instance, where a bird spends the winter is a combination of genetic programming and learned behavior. Some young birds may know instinctively how long they must fly from the breeding area to the winter area but learn the proper direction from mature birds. It isn't unusual for a bird to make a mistake in direction, but research has shown that they seldom make mistakes in duration of migration. This explains why we can sometimes see birds that are very rare to our area. They migrated for a specific time, but in the wrong direction, taking them to unexpected places.

Research has shown that some birds use the stars for navigation. Young birds denied a view of the night sky during development are disoriented when it comes time to migrate.

Migratory birds somehow use the geomagnetic field of the earth as a reference "compass." German researchers found that some birds "see" this geomagnetic field through neurons that link the eye and the brain.

Long distance migrants often have special challenges to overcome. Because of the shape of the continent, many of our Idaho birds do not need to cross oceans to arrive at winter ranges even in South America. That is not the case for birds east of the Rocky Mountains. For example, the tiny ruby-throated hummingbird, weighing less than a penny, crosses the Gulf of Mexico in a 24 hour non-stop flight. The blackpoll warbler launches from

New England, flying 2,400 miles across the Atlantic Ocean in a non-stop flight to South America lasting up to 90 hours. It burns 0.6% of its fat reserves per hour in an effort that has been equated to a human running four minute miles for 80 hours.

Birds prepare for migration through hyperphagia, gorging for several weeks before migration in order to store more fat. Some birds may actually double their body weight during this time.

The reason birds migrate isn't a secret though. Most could easily stand the cold of Idaho winters but they must go where the food is, and so they seek perpetual summer by migrating.

Someday I hope to have to use my passport and a Spanish/English dictionary to follow some Idaho birds all the way to their winter range. The only difference will be that unlike the birds, I might not come back.

Gray Jays are Yearlong Residents

I was standing by my car eating a handful of trail mix when a small flock of gray jays dove in. They were interested in the trail mix, that was sure. I couldn't coax them to eat from my hand but I sprinkled a little trail mix at my feet and they immediately moved close to avail themselves of the bounty.

Probably the most endearing, if not distinguishing, characteristic of the gray jay is its fearless nature toward humans. Indeed, human activity, particularly anything to do with food, is a real attraction and it often doesn't take long for them to discover you when setting up camp or a picnic. But larceny is in their hearts and they will steal anything that looks like food and many things that don't. Its bold thievery has earned it the nicknames "camp robber" or "robber jay." However, this same boldness can mean the birds are easily coaxed in close for a good look.

The gray jay is a non-migratory resident of the pine and spruce forests along the Rocky Mountains on to the boreal forests of Canada and Alaska. In our area, they are common in Island Park, Yellowstone and Grand Teton National Parks. They are related to crows, magpies and other jays, and as such, are among the smartest of birds.

A gray jay is slightly larger than a robin with a long tail and short rounded wings and a short black beak. They are light gray on the front and back, and the tail is medium gray. The back of the head is nearly black and eyes are set in a dark gray band. And unless you are another gray jay, both sexes look alike.

Don't confuse gray jays with the larger Clark's nutcracker, which is also bedecked in shades of gray. The nutcracker has white wing patches that are lacking with the gray jay, a longer bill and is larger overall.

Gray jays have many unique adaptations to help them brave the long winters rather than migrate. For starters, they mate for life, a rarity among songbirds. When it comes time to nest, they don't have to waste energy searching for a mate (they will take a new mate if their mate is killed).

Gray jays are not food fussies. In season they will eat berries and a variety of insects. During the winter, if food is sparse, they will subsidize their menu with spruce needles and buds. However, they have a real penchant for meat and carrion. Hunters may find gray jays beating them to the kill and waiting patiently for a chance at the leftovers and they won't pass up the opportunity to attack and kill an injured mouse or dine on eggs and even nestlings of other birds.

While being food generalists help to make them adaptable to long winters, gray jays don't take any chances with potentially low food supplies. Food that is not immediately eaten is stored in cracks under bark, woodpecker holes and other stashes. They will roll the food around in their mouth to cover it with sticky saliva which helps to preserve it over the winter months and use the food stores to raise their chicks while snow still covers the ground.

Historically, we have been quick to forgive this daring and audacious forest charmer for any corruption or pilferage. Like so many of the wildlife species around us, the gray jay brings character to the forest. May there always be gray jays to steal from our camps.

Feeder Wars

The blizzard rolled in on Saturday, not unexpectedly, but with a surprising ferocity. The snow blew sideways on the stiff wind and wet ping-pong ball-sized flakes slapped into the south side of everything, plastering on a thick frosting. As the storm worsened, birds began to appear at my empty house-style feeders. There hadn't been much action around the feeders in the past several weeks and I had gotten lackadaisical about filling them.

The finch feeder, two long mesh tubes, was still full of Niger seed. I had, just this summer, put this feeder up at the suggestion of a good friend who convinced me the finches were not just spring visitors to our neighborhood. She was right. As soon as I put up the feeders, goldfinches magically appeared. But they had been sparse lately too, and I assumed they had headed for warmer climes.

I donned a coat and mud shoes and set out to make the feeders more hospitable. They were mobbed within minutes. Hungry house finches and house sparrows flocked around them. At first, it was 20, then 40 and then numbers quickly swelled to nearly 100.

Camera in hand, I sat down and watched, just for the sheer joy of it. I hoped to see a pattern, something predictable enough to allow for a decent photograph, but the movement was too frenetic. Even though I exposed over 400 images, most were relegated to the electronic scrap heap.

This was a battlefield—no, more like a street brawl. They came in waves, but really, it was every bird for itself. The winner of the moment would monopolize its side of the feeder, fending off all other attempts to share in the booty, until it too was forced off by another.

There were definite bullies, both individually and by species. The male house sparrow seemed the bad boy of the feeder, but it amused me to see that the feisty male house finches could joust with the biggest sparrows and win their turn. None remained in possession long though. And when the hordes engulfed the feeders, even the bullies had to share or risk expulsion.

While house finches and sparrows duked it out on the house-type feeders, the tube feeders swarmed with goldfinches. They shared with house finches and an occasional sparrow, but for the most part the tubes were theirs. Naturally, there were squabbles at the tubes too. But all in all, it wasn't a brawl, more like a spat between neighbors who would later visit across the fence.

On Monday, the tempest still raged. Big flakes had fractured into driven, stinging icy flecks, and the feeders rocked in the steady winds, snow encrusted on the windward side. Birds continued their occupation of my aspen tree and I refilled the feeders several times. As fast as they were emptied, I wondered just how important my little set of feeders would be in the lives of these birds throughout this storm.

I was mindful of the fact that feeding the invasive house sparrow is ecologically unsound. Their aggressive nature and procreative abilities make them serious competitors with many native species.

Tomorrow, in bright sunshine, I might feel and act differently, but today, survival may hang in the balance. So adversaries or not, when the storm descends, even house sparrows can find refuge and are welcome to a handout at my feeders.

CHAPTER FOUR

PLACES AND TIMES

The South Fork

The South Fork. Speak these three words and just about anyone in the fishing world will know you are referring to the South Fork of the Snake River, the reason Idaho Falls consistently lands on everyone's list as one of the best places in the country to live.

Fishing is the major allure of the river. Anywhere fishing aficionados gather, talk of river flows, hatches, boats, and tackle are sure to center around the South Fork. She has become a siren mistress, stealing men away from familial duties and possibly wreaking havoc on more than one marriage. I know a number of men who spend 50 to 100 days a year on this river alone. Vice-presidents and billionaires have been succored by its waters.

But the South Fork appeals to more than fishermen. It begins at the south end of Yellowstone National Park flowing placidly beneath the Teton peaks, and attracts photographers by the score. Schwaubacher Landing and Oxbow Bend are two of the most photographed locations in the West.

Once the Snake enters the canyon west of Jackson though, its character changes. The canyon is wild and rugged, appealing to adventurers anxious to pit themselves against world-class whitewater in rapids with names like Lunchcounter and Kahuna.

The river is tamed from Alpine to the Palisades Dam by Palisades Reservoir and offers waterskiing and camping. It leaves the dam somewhat fettered, but works to regain its wild identity as it gains distance from its captor. Here begins the section all of Eastern Idaho, indeed, the world, refers to as simply, the South Fork.

With its wide cottonwood bottoms and thick willow sandbars, entering the South Fork corridor is like stepping into a wildlife Nirvana. From mink to moose and orioles to osprey, wildlife above the water is just as exciting as the fishing beneath. For the observant, every corner, every cottonwood grove, the sky above, and even the river bank, is loaded with wildlife.

There is a great blue heron rookery, if you know where to look, and peregrines ply the skies. Beaver calmly eat their twigs as you float by, or, conversely, slap a warning with their tail if your drift catches them off-guard. The ensuing splash and crash sound like a breaching salmon.

Moose, elk, white-tailed deer, and mule deer can all be seen swimming in the river or moving like ghosts along the banks. They live here, among the cottonwood and willow jungles, judged one of the most important habitats in the nation, rarely seen except from the river itself.

Just last week, a pair of sandhill cranes landed near me as I stood on a spit of gravel, rod in hand. As I cast, I followed their progress toward the river by listening to their washboard cries well before I could spot them; all wings, necks and legs gliding in for at least a quarter mile without a single wingbeat. We shared the shoreline for awhile, until they disappeared behind a line of willows.

As I fished, cedar waxwings and goldfinches darted about. Canada geese honked from shore and mallards flushed from the edges. A raft of white pelicans ignored me and floated nearby until pea-sized hail made all of us duck our heads and run for cover.

Overhead, an osprey and several bald eagles patrolled the skies and, like me, searched the river for fish. A kingfisher worked near shore. And avian fishermen were not my only competitors that day. Mink and otter also ply the waters and when I kept a rainbow trout, I guarded it carefully.

And that was a rather average day. Even a short trip on the South Fork yields a plethora of wildlife. And it only gets better when the fish are biting.

Exploring Close to Home

When a camping trip fell through a couple of weeks ago, my wife, Cathy, suggested we day hike to the Wind Caves in Darby Canyon near Victor. She had been to the Wind Caves before with a group of teenage girls, but for some reason, I had never made the time.

In less than four hours from our door, we were standing inside the hundred-foot-tall opening to the cave. It was evident that earlier in the season the stream that now trickled from the cave was an impressive torrent. We explored deep inside until claustrophobia and a definite chill drew us back toward the sunshine.

The day was well spent and I quietly wondered why it had taken me years to make that hike.

Last weekend, I re-paid Cathy. With the help of my son and his jet boat, Cathy experienced the South Fork of the Snake River for the first time. She was thrilled to catch her first brown trout and to see the beautiful canyon section of river only visible by boat. Separated from Highway 26 by Antelope Flat, she had never even realized it was there.

Throughout much of the day, Cathy chided, "Why haven't you ever brought me up here?" That evening, at a BBQ, she told anyone who would listen that it was unbelievable that in 16 years living in Eastern Idaho, her schmuck husband had never taken her on the river.

She was right: it was a pathetic situation and my defense was weak. I did remind her that it was hard to fit a family of seven in a drift boat and big jet boats were expensive. Really though, despite the fact the South Fork is, figuratively, right outside our door, I just never made it a priority.

I've traveled thousands of miles to find wildlife and wilderness experiences. In all of those travels, I realized I had driven through or flown over some of the most incredible country in the world, right in my own "backyard", by-passing it for "greener" pastures.

Thus, I decided to methodically investigate what I had been missing. With my DeLorme *Idaho Atlas and Gazetteer* in hand, I drew three concentric circles on the map. The circles represented 50, 100, and 150 mile radii (100, 200 and 300 mile diameters) from my house.

The 50 mile circle (7,850 square miles if I did the math correctly, $pi(r^2)$) included dozens of places that either I had never been to or that needed more thorough exploration. It included places like Hells Half Acre, the St. Anthony

Sand Dunes, a long stretch of the Henrys Fork, the South Fork and the main Snake River, Menan Buttes and the Big Hole, Palisades, and Caribou mountain ranges. There were seven wildlife management areas, Camas and Grays Lake National Wildlife Refuges, many miles of streams, several reservoirs, and hundreds of miles of hiking trails.

The amount of territory that I had not carefully explored within the 100 mile circle (31,400 square miles) was mind boggling and included three National Parks/Monuments, each of which could take years to completely investigate. Red Rock, Minidoka, and Bear Lake National Wildlife Refuges, Harriman State Park, Henrys Lake, Island Park Reservoir, the Lemhi and Big Lost mountains, including Mt. Borah, at least two ski resorts, and Montana's Hebgen Lake were also all at least partially inside this circle.

But that was nothing compared to the 150 mile circle (70,650 square miles!). There was enough fantastic country between the 100 and 150 mile circles to keep me occupied for several lifetimes.

It was proof enough that I didn't have to roam another continent to find plenty to explore. And, with gas pinging off the three dollar mark, exploring these close-to-home areas is as practical as it is beneficial. It turns out that it is simply a matter of recognizing the treasures in our own backyard.

Iowa isn't Idaho but—Surprise!—it isn't Hell Either

I once visited with an older woman who proudly proclaimed that with the exception of an occasional dreaded one hour trip to Idaho Falls, she had never set foot outside her county. Now, granted, the county she lives in is a wonderful place, a vacation destination for many thousands of people each year. There is a lot to do and see, but I can't help but believe that she is the poorer for not seeing some of the rest of the world outside this corner of eastern Idaho.

There was a time when I too would have seen no reason to venture, in my case, east of the Rocky Mountains. I was sure at that time that the "East" held nothing of interest for a self proclaimed true wilderness wanderer like me. Iowa, nothing but cornfields and people in my view, was surely the epicenter of a world with which I had no reason to connect; a view I held for a long time.

I first realized my narrow-sightedness as we drove a circuitous route back from Memphis, Tennessee, several years ago. We crossed Iowa in the evening and found it anything but flat and uninteresting. Certainly, there were no mountains in view, but the scenic byway we followed chased across rolling terrain draped in shades of green, over rivers and streams, and through wooded dells. It wasn't at all like I had expected. In fact, we thoroughly enjoyed the drive.

I am writing this in Des Moines, Iowa. Nowadays, we find ourselves here once or twice a year visiting a couple of very special granddaughters. I never expected to routinely visit this place, but I have found it far more fascinating than I had supposed. Certainly, it is not wild like the Selkirk or White Cloud Mountains, but it does have charms of its own.

Wildlife seems to be everywhere, including deep into the suburbs. My son routinely sees white-tailed deer as he rides his bike to campus. Turkeys strut in the open fields on the outskirts of town. Cottontail rabbits, raccoons, opossums, and fox squirrels are common in most yards; sometimes becoming pesky, but almost always entertaining.

The first thing we did when we arrived was to buy our son's family a bird feeder and a sack of feed. Compared to home, there is an entirely different suite of songbirds to grace the new feeder. Cardinals and grackles have already found it and with one day left before we head home, we are hoping to see even more.

Although Iowa probably has the distinction of being the most intensively agricultural state, even here there are still nine national wildlife refuges and a National Monument. And Iowa has something the interior West will never have: water. Rain doesn't fall, it comes in deluges, sometimes six inches in a single storm, and streams and rivers are everywhere. Trees and prairie spring up spontaneously whenever the plow is stilled, and natural parks and woodlands line the rivers, even through the cities.

Although it isn't Idaho, there is more to appreciate in Iowa than I ever imagined. Isn't that the way of life, though? Whether with places or people, if we just dare to venture outside our "county," we find the bigger world is fascinating, not frightening. It just takes that first step.

Lake Bonneville Flood

Almost 15,000 years ago, ancient Lake Bonneville lapped peacefully at its shores at the highest pool level it ever attained. With an elevation of 5,090 feet and a maximum depth of over 1,000 feet, it was a monster of a lake, stretching nearly from what would be Downey, Idaho to south of Sevier, Utah and covering over 20,000 square miles. Its shoreline, if straightened, would have reached from Downey to New Orleans.

The lake was controlled by a dam of coalesced gravels from alluvial deposits. It sat like a cork in a bottle from Red Rock Pass to Zenda (between Downey and Preston). Maybe it was an earthquake, or just water piping through the dam that caused it to weaken, but sometime around 14,500 years ago, the dam failed, spilling water north. The flood forever changed the character of the Portnuef Valley from Marsh Creek to American Falls and the Snake River from American Falls to Lewiston.

When the dam collapsed, one million cubic meters of water *per second*— enough to fill the Empire State Building each second— rushed through the gap and began sluicing off the gravel down to bedrock. In comparison, this flood was 33 times larger than the peak discharge of the Teton Dam failure, seven times more volume than the Amazon River, and 500 times more than the highest flows ever recorded for the Snake River at Idaho Falls.

For about two months, the flood continued at this incredible rate as the lake volume shrank. About a year after initial failure, the lake finally achieved a new equilibrium, 350 feet lower, when it reached the bedrock level in Red Rock Pass.

The surging waters, in volumes almost impossible to imagine, had a dramatic impact on the landscape. Incredible force accompanied the raging flood as it slashed through the country at 60 miles per hour and up to 300 feet deep. Volcanic basalt walls crumbled before it. Chunks of this rough-edged basalt tumbled downstream and within a few miles became smooth stones that would later be deposited far from today's river channel as the water slowed or changed course.

Residents of Pocatello and Twin Falls would later call these huge oval boulders petrified melons and the name would stick. Melon gravel bars up to 300 feet deep and a mile and a half wide are still apparent, reminders of the tremendous force that shaped them.

As gravel deposits built and eroded, the river surge changed course repeatedly, creating some of the most unique features to persist today. New channels were cut, several miles long and 150 feet deep, cavernous 100 foot deep potholes were scoured as water whirled and swirled as if in a clothes washer. Waterfalls peeled off more basalt and the scouring water polished and fluted the newly exposed stone. Once waters receded, these new features were left as dry reminders of the flood.

Gravels were deposited in slackwaters, eddies, and other areas where water slowed its frenetic pace. The town of Chubbuck and the Pocatello Airport both rest on a Lake Bonneville floodwater delta. Further downstream, gravel bars continued to build and re-shape the river all the way to Lewiston.

Lake Bonneville stayed at its new level for thousands more years, but eventually, it shrank to a mere puddle we now call the Great Salt Lake. The Queen of Lakes was gone, but when you stop to look, you can read her memoirs everywhere along the Snake River.

No Wasted Moments

My sons, a friend, and I went into the mountains in Island Park with the intent of quickly finding and harvesting a large bull elk. I had seen many during my previous archery hunting seasons and this time I had a coveted rifle permit. But day one foreshadowed an ominous omen when bulls refused to bugle and scorned our imitation cow calls. It quickly shaped up to be a long hard week of hunting.

As we hunted through days that found us far up the hill before sunrise and walking back to camp well after dark, we battled with a discouragement it seems only a hunter can know. The time wasn't wasted though. Each hour brought something new and wonderful, it just wasn't elk.

On three different occasions, beautiful pine marten, yellow chested and a rich dark brown on top, came to within a few feet of us. Each time, it was the same dance. They would race part way up a tree and then peer around the trunk at the strange apparitions that we must have been. Then they darted away only to return and eye us again. Their curiosity gave us a close-up glance at their grace and charm that we would never have seen if we hadn't been immersed in the woods.

Twice I met up with a great gray owl. Each time it caught my attention as it flew noiselessly from one perch to the next. It was not shy and afforded me a grand experience. While in its presence, I forgot my appointment at the elk watering hole and observed it as long as it allowed.

In the pre-dawn one morning, sitting on the edge of a clearcut hoping to waylay a bull, a sparrow-sized bird mistook me for a tree and landed briefly on my shoulder. Moments later it flew to my friend, landing on his hat, and then squabbled with another of its kind for possession of a bush. No elk to ambush but the morning wasn't a waste.

On a long evening hike near the border of Yellowstone Park, we encountered large canine tracks. Using a rifle cartridge for a measuring tool, I determined that the tracks belonged to a wolf. My competition true, but also an amazing creature and skillful predator. Just knowing it was hunting here gave us a shot of hope.

One morning, a mule deer buck approached to within five yards of my friend, stared at him as he sat motionless with his back to a huge Douglas fir, then it resumed eating and slowly walked away. On another occasion, another mule deer buck wandered into camp and drank from the stream ten yards from the trailer.

We talked of the coyotes. At the first of the week, the howling began after midnight, but as the moon waned, their howling started progressively earlier. Each morning we found coyote tracks as we hunted and speculated whether they were "our coyotes".

Most importantly, my sons and I spent time together in a place where walls crumble and fathers and sons can bond. That alone was worth the week.

On the last day of our hunt, my son, Casey, did harvest a nice bull. It fulfilled the purpose of our time in the woods and gave us a real sense of accomplishment. But the week was already a success, and had been from the start. There is no such thing as a waste of time when it is shared with family, friends, and nature.

Decisions

My anxiety began several weeks ago. I poured over maps and old photos of backpacking destinations from the past and Google-Earthed new ones. Family obligations had precluded our annual trip last season and I had been pining and whining for a year and I was determined to choose well. As the time drew near, though, I was pensive and indecisive. I was ready to hit the trail, but which trail? I would only get one trip this summer and I wanted it to be perfect.

So, this was a serious decision for me. First, there were practical considerations. Several of us were out of shape meaning that deep incursions into the back country were out of the question, but I still wanted all the adventure I could find.

The dilemma came down to two choices: should we visit a new and uncharted (for us) area or return to someplace I knew fairly intimately?

The arguments were strong in both camps. Exploring a new area where every rise in the trail brings a new and exciting vista keeps every sense fully engaged. Better still, the anticipation of what "might be" can keep me up at night. Would the lakes be full of two-pound trout? Perhaps the sunrises would be the best I have ever seen. Mystery. That is what new trails are all about.

On the other hand, familiarity in the mountains seldom breeds contempt. I know where the best places are for photographs and which lakes have what kind of fish. I know the trails and the back ways. Familiar with the big picture, I am free to explore. Again, mystery rules but, it is discovery at a much more intimate level.

Although I had been four times up the trail I finally chose, my decision to return to Big Boulder Creek in the Boulder/White Clouds near Challis, was made because of a love of the place. Going back, I knew I would relive many wonderful experiences, times with my sons and with friends. In this sense, reminiscing would add to the experience and lengthen the perceived time afield.

Even better, on this trip, I would also finally get to share this special place with my wife and oldest son. For myriad reasons, neither one had been able to make previous trips and I looked forward to telling my wife, "see that peak there? That is the one Casey, Zack and I climbed". And I could tell my son, an ardent fisherman, "The fishing is best in that lake over there. A double humpy will knock'em dead".

I have visited the lion's share of the nearly 50 lakes on the USGS quad that contains our destination. One basin still eludes me. Since I have made my decision, I have stared at the map and schemed how I could get there later this summer. But the trail is long and the prospect of being in better shape in short order is modest. It may wait until next year. But then, it isn't going anywhere and the anticipation is half the fun.

New Places

As I write this, my backpack sits on the floor next to me. My wife, Cathy, and youngest son, Zack, are busy gathering gear and preparing food for a pilgrimage that begins tomorrow and will stretch across seven glorious days. This adventure will take us into a corner of the world where the trails are unknown to our boots. Within the week I hope we are at least partially familiar with this vast area that will take a lifetime to explore at a rate of one week a summer.

I must admit that the decision to break from the familiar White Cloud Mountains and what has become an annual trek there did not come easily. Returning to a familiar and enchanting place year after year has many appeals.

First, since Cathy has not always accompanied me on these trips, I can share with her all the treasures I have discovered and recount stories authoritatively. "See that big pointed rock up there? That is the one that Ben climbed. Remember seeing the picture of him with Castle Peak in the background?"

Second, because everything is familiar, the GPS, compass and even the map could all stay at home. We know the route to trail-less Gunsight Lake, the back way from Island Lake to Cove Lake, and the trail over Windy Devil Saddle and the cross-country scramble down to Quiet Lake.

We have climbed and named the unnamed peaks, swum in the lakes, weathered storms, and thrilled to sunrises over quiet waters. It seems that every meadow, glade, and weathered ridge liberates a memory. In a word, even though the place is wild, it is comfortable.

Just last weekend we learned the value of pushing ourselves on a three day trip into a new corner of the White Clouds. This was Cathy's introduction to rock scrambling, working straight up a rocky chute that separated Born Lakes from Four Basin Lakes. For Zack and me, it was just another climb, but to Cathy, it was Everest without oxygen. I doubt the images will soon fade of her spider crawling up the rocks with Zack bounding up from rock to rock to help her.

Nonetheless, she appreciated (once back at camp) the fact that she had met a challenge; she had dared the mountain and had survived. Several fine sermons about the episode were later tested on Zack and me as she drew analogies to life of her experiences with fear, endurance, and testing her limits.

And, I guess, that is part of the reason we are choosing to point our boots in a different direction. It is not that we are tired of the old and familiar—I doubt I will ever tire of the White Clouds, but the need to try a new challenge, to see the world from a different perspective is strong. It is time to feel the tingle of uneasiness a new challenge brings, to again test our skills, and re-engage senses that lay latent in familiar territory. This new place, the Wind Rivers of Wyoming, is huge country, brimming with trout-filled lakes, granite peaks, and the occasional grizzly bear. It is a country that will challenge us with steep grades, test navigation skills, and reward us with scenery unsurpassed anywhere in the world.

So, off we go, looking for another new place that in time we hope will become a familiar old place. We may be tested by mountains, weather, bear encounters, or poor fishing, but one thing that I doubt will be missing is adventure. And that is part of what life seems to be about—finding your own adventure.

April is the Month of Renewal

The empty promises of March were just too much for me, so I escaped—it was long-sleeved shirt weather at Lake Powell in southern Utah and that was a welcome relief from eastern Idaho's bitter chill. When I returned to Idaho, temperatures were still in the low 30's and there were traces of fresh snow on the shady side of the house. However, blooming crocuses ringed my aspens and were a triumphant symbol that the backbone of winter had finally been broken.

Animals, too, are celebrating as spring begins to shoulder its way through winter's door. Indeed, April is as incredibly full of wildlife activity as March was a void.

Big game animals, after a prolonged and difficult winter, are beginning to find green forage, recovering precious energy and moving back toward summer ranges. They are readily seen in fields and hillsides. Be extra careful on the highways for the next several months.

Snow geese are piling up at Mud Lake, Camas National Wildlife Refuge, and Market lake Wildlife Management Area (WMA). Along with the sandhill cranes, they seem to pull spring weather up with them as they migrate north for the summer. A single flock of geese may have ten thousand or more individuals and when they take to the air en masse, the roar of wings wraps around you like a shawl.

On the roadsides, yellow-belly marmots are putting on a show. Awake from a long winter's nap, they are making up for lost time. Snakes will join them, attracted to the solar energy stored in the roads' dark surfaces. Again, for all their sakes, be careful on the roads.

April is a major month for birds and for birdwatchers. Sage-grouse are doing the grouse two-step right now. Sharp-tailed grouse will be dancing up a storm by the end of the month as well. Be aware that only early risers are invited to the performances; they are winding down two hours after sunrise. If you want to really get involved with the grouse, consider participating in Grouse Days, in Dubois, ID (www.duboisidaho.com).

At places like Market Lake and Mud Lake, dozens of species of waterfowl, wading birds, shorebirds, and songbirds are all in breeding plumage, fighting for territories and attracting mates. All the activity and clamor can leave you dizzy.

Further up into the hills, black bears and grizzly bears are emerging from their winter dens. They are hungry and lean after a winter's fast and will wander in search of the carrion of animals unlucky enough to perish during winter. As soon as the roads open in Yellowstone National Park (usually about the third weekend of April), anywhere from Mammoth to LaMar Valley and through Hayden Valley can be great places for a bear show.

April is the turning point for most birds and animals. It is the stage in their yearly cycle where they switch from surviving to thriving, build nests and prepare for offspring.

Just as surely as March is still winter, April is spring, the season of birth and rebirth. Of course, there will be spats of nastiness as winter usually refuses to "go quietly into the night". But, wildlife has rebuffed winter's mauling—toughing it out, escaping or sleeping it away, and the botanical world is waking up. The world is as it should be and all of nature is rewarded for its resolve.

New Places Equal New Critters

My wife and I just completed a whirlwind trip taking our daughter and her husband back to Memphis, Tennessee to attend graduate school. We covered over 4,000 miles and passed through 14 states in seven days. Unfortunately, the vast majority of the trip was windshield time with little opportunity to sightsee or scout for wildlife off the beaten track.

Even then, we saw the standard wildlife from the highways: jackrabbits, white-tailed and mule deer, turkeys, pronghorn and marmots. We even saw some of the less common species such as bison, bighorn sheep and mountain goats when we visited Custer State Park in the Black Hills of South Dakota.

What thrilled me the most, though, were the critters I have always heard about but have never seen (at least outside a zoo).

For example, one of the wildlife highlights of the trip was seeing armadillos and opossums. Okay, I will admit right here and now that I only saw these two species as road-kill. Texas, Oklahoma, and Arkansas were real killing grounds for these species, so the body count was high enough that I decided they counted for me.

It was after dark when we pulled into our hotel in St. Louis, Missouri. As I walked past the lighted pool, a flurry of activity in the pool drew me in. At first, I thought it might be a bat but as I moved closer, I saw a huge moth was drowning.

With a buoy on a rope, I rescued the first Luna moth I had ever seen. As I held its soggy body, Cathy and I admired its beautiful palm-sized pale green wings and pearl white body. It slowly flapped those giant wings, and when it had sufficiently dried, I gently released it on a nearby shrub. In the morning, I was gratified to see it was still clinging to the bushes near the pool.

In Nauvoo, Illinois, the state bird of Illinois, Indiana, Kentucky, Ohio, North Carolina, Virginia, and West Virginia nearly caused me to wreck the truck. I have seen pictures of the brilliant red cardinal but until then had never seen one of these eastern birds. I completely forgot that I was driving when this beautiful male cardinal flew to the side of the road and I nearly followed it, truck and all, into the thicket.

Somewhere along the trail, I found another critter whose acquaintance I probably could have done without. While showering one evening, I found that a deer tick (as opposed to the wood ticks we have out West) had embedded itself into my shoulder. These ticks are very small but carry Lyme disease. I am so excited.

I have friends who think I shouldn't get excited about mere rodents, but when we found real prairie dogs and an entire prairie dog town in South Dakota, I slammed on the brakes. Prairie dogs and their towns were once keystone species on the prairies, routinely turning soil and aiding in water percolation that then fueled the abundant grasses bison, pronghorn, and elk thrived on. They were not mere rodents and having the chance to actually see them was a thrill.

Someday I hope to travel to exotic places to witness wildlife events that I have only seen on the Nature Channel. Until then, our 4,000 mile tour reminded me that I could spend a lifetime exploring my own country and never see all the wildlife it has to offer.

Mount Everest Virtual Tour

I am on a Google Earth kick, and decided to visit someplace that is very interesting, but where I am confident I will never visit. It wasn't hard to decide on Mount Everest because I know two people who have made it to Base Camp, but I am sure I will never go even that far.

My Google Earth tour was impressive. I explored views from the summit and investigated every angle and route. I spun around the peak until I was nearly airsick. Between Google Earth, the internet, and knowing people who have been to Base Camp, I am now a self proclaimed expert.

Everest was officially recognized as the world's tallest peak following the Great Trigonometrical Survey of India in 1852. Until then, it was just another Himalayan peak known as Peak XV. In 1865, it was officially named after Sir George Everest, the British surveyor-general of India.

However, Tibet and Nepal, the two countries that share Everest, have long recognized the pre-eminence of this big hunk of ice-covered rock. In Nepalese the mountain is called Sagarmatha, meaning, goddess of the sky. In Tibetan it is known as, Chomolungma, meaning, mother goddess of the universe.

In 1954, the elevation of Everest was set at 29,028 feet. However, with the more accurate Global Positioning System technology of today, the elevation was revised to 29,035 feet in 1999. Even then, it is still growing at four millimeters a year—about three quarters of an inch in 20 years.

Serious attempts at climbing the mountain did not begin until 1921. The first modern tragedy occurred on June 8, 1924. George Mallory and Andrew Irvine disappeared during an attempted ascent. Mallory's body was discovered in 1999 but Irvine's has never been found. Debate still rages about whether or not they reached the top.

During the next 29 years, there were ten additional expeditions to conquer the mountain but each failed. Edmund Hillary and Tenzing Norgay were the first to officially summit the top of the world on May 29, 1953.

Everest is a dangerous place. According to <u>Everest News,</u> as of Dec. 31st 2004, 168 people had died on the mountain. On the bright side though, over 2200 have made the summit.

The climb is risky business and may be less esthetic than we flatlanders might imagine. Those that die on the mountain may be left where they fall and exhausted climbers often abandon gear. Rather than a serene pitting of man against mountain, an ascent is often a ghoulish hike through litter, old camps, and frozen corpses.

Avalanches are the number one killer on the mountain. However, enter the Death Zone above 25,000 feet, and anything can happen. Temperatures can plunge to -40°F in minutes, and winds can charge at 125 miles per hour. Violent sudden storms may sweep a climber into a crevasse or off a cliff.

Physiologically, it is even more dangerous. There is two-thirds less oxygen at 25,000 feet than there is at sea level. Because of this, altitude sickness, the deadly build-up of fluids in the lungs, and the swelling of an oxygen-deprived brain, is an ever present danger, along with hypothermia and frostbite. Subsequent loss of good judgment ability and hallucinations add to the danger.

Dead bodies, lethal avalanches, thin air. I don't think I've lost my spirit of adventure, but on this one I am happy to take the virtual tour.

Camping on Public Land

My daughter and her family won't be going camping this Memorial Day weekend. It isn't that they don't want to—Beth loves to camp and wants to introduce her two girls to a family tradition that reaches back several generations. But they live in Knoxville, Tennessee, and although there are national forests, state parks and Great Smoky National Park all within a few hours' drive, they didn't think to reserve a campsite and now all available sites are full. For them, camping will have to wait.

A world such as that is almost impossible for Idahoans to imagine. Why, we can point our vehicle in just about any direction and, within a few minutes, we can be on public ground where we are welcome to pitch a tent and stay for up to fourteen days. Sure, we bring our own water and haul our own trash back out, but judging from Beth's experience, that is a small price for the freedom that is ours.

Even here, the world is changing and we are seeing more places where camping space is at a premium. I can still remember the day when Yellowstone National Park was anticipating a million visitors a year. I thought it was crowded then. Now, with three million visitors each year, camping by reservation is the only way to be sure of a campsite in the park during the summer months.

We have a few other areas where demand can exceed available space or, in order to preserve the quality of an area, use is limited. The float portion of the South Fork of the Snake River comes to mind. There, camping is only allowed in designated areas which limit the number of campers on the river at any one time. This protects both the resource and the wild character this stretch of river is renowned for.

There are a few campgrounds that are so popular that getting a site is the equivalent to winning the lottery. I have never passed the turn-off to Coffee Pot Campground in Island Park when the "Campground Full" sign wasn't up and Henrys Lake on Memorial Day weekend is not for the faint of heart.

But no matter. There are a million places to camp—just pull off the road almost anywhere. In fact, our favorite campsites have always been the undeveloped sites where there are no neighbors or fees and we can sing around the campfire until midnight if we want to.

This is an incredible treasure, but is so common we likely take it for granted. We don't recognize that at one time, Easterners enjoyed the same freedom. Unfortunately, though, there is a direct inverse relationship between population growth and unfettered opportunity to recreate on public ground. Even here in the West, there can come a time when, without regulation, humans seeking nature may kill the very thing they love. For instance, I grew up wandering in Mill Creek Canyon just east of Salt Lake City. Today, the number of recreationists that can enter the canyon each day is limited and a fee is charged.

We still have time to help direct the character of camping recreation for future generations. Much of that will depend on how we treat the public lands that support us. Treat them as the gems they are and the welcome mat will be out much longer. Regard them as the neighborhood vacant lot and someday we'll think we are in Tennessee.

Mountain Lakes

On a long and beautiful drive across central Idaho last week, I was in awe of the outdoor recreational opportunities in Idaho. Rafters and kayakers, bicyclists, fishermen, hikers, and horseback riders seemed to be everywhere.

Everyone, it seems, has a favorite activity in the out-of-doors or some special place where they would like to spend all their days. For some, rivers are like Mother Earth herself beckoning. Whether it is a kayak or raft ride through crashing rapids, or fishing the quiet eddies, they just can't seem to get enough of the flowing water.

For others, it's the desert. There is almost a genetic connection for a few, but for most desert rats, the desert slowly sifts into their bloodstream like fine drifting sand and becomes part of them. The quiet, the solitude, the wide open country is their vision quest.

The challenge of the peaks and cliffs proves irresistible to many. You find them hiking every trail, ropes dangling over their shoulders, pitons clanging on their belts, as they head for their personal vertical limit or another peak.

For some it is the rush of adrenaline or perhaps a brush with death that helps them to realize they are really alive. Others seek serenity and a chance to leave the tumult of civilization behind. Still others mix favorite activities with the outdoors, enhancing both experiences. They hike for the sheer joy of it, ride horses or bicycle in beautiful places, or crawl through caves into earth's depths where mountaineering skills are often needed.

I have tried and prize all these activities. I've treasured the view from the top of the Grand Teton and braved the 100-foot free rappel. I've sucked in a bellyful of the Salmon River when my kayak refused to complete a belly roll, packed with horses into the wilderness, and stood ankle deep in icy water while my light plied in the blackness of a cave. I love the desert, rivers, and mountain peaks. Given enough time, I'd do it all, spend time in them all.

But recreational time is scant during the short summer months. I have to choose my activities carefully, knowing full well that to choose one pursuit is to forego another.

That's why high mountain lakes are always at the end of my trail. I am drawn to them like a child to a cookie jar. I am especially enthralled with lakes shoved up tight in a cirque basin with cliffs and scree, boulders and ice all around. Forced to choose between all the possible outdoor pursuits, I gravitate unerringly to mountain lakes. On foot, horseback, or even by car when I can, I hope to see them all.

To some, one lake is the same as another. Not to me. Each is a gem with a character all its own, often a character discovered only after spending several nights on its shores and rising early to photograph the sunrise reflecting from its still waters. While I have my favorites, I have never found a lake I couldn't embrace. All embody a peace and serenity I find nowhere else.

One of my favorite lakes is Sapphire Lake in Big Boulder Creek of the Boulder/White Cloud Mountains. Standing on its shores, it is indeed the color of the gem, sapphire. Idaho may be called the Gem State because of an abundance of precious stones. But thousands of mountain lakes sparkle in the high country—granite jewelry studded with gems of another kind far more beautiful than precious stones.

To achieve my goal of seeing every mountain lake from Stanley to the Wyoming line, I might have to decline opportunities to float the South Fork or bag another peak. And those choices are painful. But, when I have completed the goal and have seen every lake, for me, the sacrifice will have been worth it.

Bosque Del Apache

Bosque Del Apache National Wildlife Refuge, Socorro, New Mexico. The rising sun dueled with the cloud cover on this cold January morning, thrusting daggers of amber light through every weakness and illuminating the surface of the shallow pond. The orange reflections silhouetted thousands of snow geese and sandhill cranes. Additional waves of birds continually appeared from the horizon and settled in to join the already teeming and vociferous throng.

We had been shivering on the bank for well over an hour, waiting for the single unpredictable and magical moment aptly called, "fly-out". Finally, a warning of imminent action was signaled by a dramatic crescendo in their cacophony. Then, with a deafening roar of wings, virtually every goose and crane on the huge pond was airborne. The horizon went black as this mass of birds set course for the day's feeding grounds. The best show of the day had just drawn to a magnificent climax and we joined several dozen other onlookers heading back to our cars and heaters.

Fly-out was repeated less dramatically in reverse with the evening fly-in, as birds returned from the fields to spend the night in the security of the water. Wave followed wave as geese, flying high, circled and descended by the hundreds. Until dark there was a constant re-positioning as a thousand snow geese here or two thousand there suddenly rose up in discontent, circled the pond and boisterously settled back in. Cranes came in from all directions and we felt like we were in the center of the universe.

In between fly-out and fly-in was the rest of the day. With so much to see, the days were challenging. We slowly prowled the 15 mile long auto tour loop around the marshes hunting for photo-ops, explored the visitor center and hiked the Refuge trails up sandy canyons.

Things weren't always this rosy. By the time Bosque Del Apache was formed as a wildlife refuge in 1939, the heart of the refuge had been tamed by upstream dams and irrigation diversions. The Rio Grande had once been an unruly river, flooding the wetlands each spring when it overran its banks. Periodic massive flooding would even change the course of the river. In short, the entire system was maintained by the temper tantrums of the Rio Grande. With the loss of this yearly renewal, wildlife value diminished and in 1939, only 17 cranes and 30 snow geese called Bosque home for the winter.

Massive habitat engineering projects have since returned some of the ground back to a semblance of the natural system. Over 9,000 acres of the 57,000 acre Refuge are under this intensive management. Another 30,000 acres are protected as designated wilderness. Management and protection seem to have worked. During our visit, 12,000 cranes and 30,000 snow geese were happily crowded onto the refuge.

Bosque had long been on my list of must-see places, but, unless you are a bird watcher or a photographer, you may never have heard of it. After one visit, though, you won't forget it. News commentator Charles Kuralt frequently visited there because Bosque Del Apache and the sandhill cranes, "got into my soul."

The effect is strong, too. On one hike, we met a woman named Elizabeth Crane. I expressed typical Yankee skepticism at her name, in this place. She promptly pulled out her driver's license: Elizabeth W. Crane. After retiring from teaching in Ohio, she moved to Socorro to be near the birds and promptly changed her name to reflect how she felt about it. And the W.? "Stands for Whooping. The gal at the courthouse talked me into just the initial."

Seldom is pandemonium soothing to my soul. But the ceaseless ruckus at Bosque serves as more than a tonic. In a time when we suffer from the toxin of civilization, Bosque, incessant and overpowering, serves as a massively administered natural antidote. When progress begins to overwhelm me this year, I'm headed back to the Bosque for another dose.

CHAPTER FIVE

PEOPLE OUTDOORS

People We Have Met

I have never been accused of being a social butterfly. In fact, more than a few people have commented to my wife that the mug shot that accompanies some of my columns makes me look gruff and mean—an image I haven't gone out of my way to dispel. However, when I am outdoors, my personality must undergo a shift. My innate reserved nature fades, and I really enjoy meeting people who share a common interest or who have a unique story or perspective.

As a sometime photographer, I am always interested in other photographers—not just their gear and techniques but also their stories, which are often colorful and occasionally truthful. They are a clannish bunch, given to talk of f-stops, shutter speeds and perfect light, and are usually found in large groups at unique photo-ops such as a grizzly bear sighting. We will stand around, waiting for the perfect shot and talk of places we have been and recent conquests and lucky breaks—such as photographing a bighorn ram right from the road. Conversation is sporadic, interrupted with click, whir and wind as hundreds of frames of film glide by shutters when our current subject does something out of the ordinary. I rarely remember for long the names of people I encounter (yet another personality glitch) but when I do, I anxiously look for their bylines in magazines and mentally cheer when I find one.

The most famous photographers I have ever met in the field, two of my heroes, were Leonard Lee Rue III and his son, Len Rue. We visited while we watched a bull elk. Frankly, I lost interest in the elk and turned my camera on Leonard Rue, figuring he was the best trophy I would capture that day. I actually gave them a business card and offered to be their tour guide should they ever come to Idaho. Our encounter was brief but memorable (at least for me). I have since added Donald M. Jones to my list after a chance encounter at a trailhead in Glacier National Park.

Then there are the retired couples who spend their time bouncing from park to park or who make yearly pilgrimages to a particular park. These folks are often a wealth of knowledge about "their" parks and offer great tips on the best wildlife or scenic wonders. One Colorado couple my wife and I met last summer gave us the recent history of a grizzly sow and three cubs we were watching near Soda Butte in Yellowstone. They shared digital images of the sow, lying on her back in the middle of the road nursing her cubs. I was impressed and jealous.

They also pointed out some mountain goats we never would have seen without their assistance.

We hiked briefly with the Bachelor family in Great Smoky National Park. They have been camping at Catalahooche for about 30 years and recounted that when they first began visiting the park, they would camp alongside the children of some of the original owners of the property. They regaled the Bachelors with stories of growing up in the land before it was a national park.

With the return of the wolves to Yellowstone, another group has evolved into a culture. These are the wolf and grizzly bear followers, usually found between Slough Creek and Soda Butte in Lamar Valley. These people demonstrate a patience that would have Job wiggling in his seat as they glass distant slopes. They know many of the animals by their radio collar number and are often in communication with friends via portable radios. They are fascinating to talk to and are a real conduit to the wolf and grizzly action.

Each of us has a reason to be outdoors and each of us has a story and a perspective. Hearing them around the campfire or on the trail is an important human connection that enhances the natural experience.

Smart Phone Apps for Nature

Although the bird in my binoculars looked familiar, I couldn't place it. Definitely in the sparrow family, but the yellow head stripes were confusing. I reached for my smart phone, touched the Audubon Guide application and searched the sparrow family. In seconds, I was sure I had my answer; nevertheless, I browsed all four photos and listened to a recording of its song, and then checked the description and range for verification. Yup, a savannah sparrow. It was familiar because I had photographed one in Florida several months earlier.

It was so EASY. Everything I needed for identification was right there on an application, app for short, that I had downloaded to my phone for $10, less than the cost of a paperback field guide. With over 700 species, multiple photos, voice identification, and the usual description and range, it is the perfect birding companion unless the phone battery dies.

At home I did a little searching at the Apps Store for other apps useful to the outdoor enthusiast. I was amazed at what I found. Since I hope to be in Alaska in June, I was immediately intrigued by Alaska Wildflower Pro for under two dollars. But that was just the beginning. I found apps for field guides for birds (including the Sibley Guide which, at $30, was by far the most expensive app I found), trees, butterflies, mammals, and tracks and scats.

There was an app that included the entire Army Survival Manual, apps on bird watching, and apps for GPS that would, among other things, enable the GPS in my phone to store multiple way points, and record tracks and trails like a regular GPS, potentially eliminating the need to carry a separate GPS unit. There were nature apps on African wildlife and arctic wildlife, and an app called High School Life Science, rated 5 stars by users. Another that caught my interest was the app called, Go Explore WYOMING. That one might find its way onto my phone sooner than later.

For the hunter and fisherman, about half the states have hunting and fishing regulation apps available for 99 cents each. While Idaho's hunting regulations are apparently currently unavailable, an entrepreneur has made the entire set of the current Idaho fishing regulations into an app. No more losing the regulations or not having a copy when you need one.

Other intriguing apps are related to game calling. There are highly rated free apps for coyote, deer, elk, duck, and goose calls. Could I turn my cell phone into a wildlife calling machine? Fascinating.

Wallpapers, books (how about a collection of Ralph Waldo Emerson or Henry David Thoreau for $2?), photos, nature-based ringtones, alarms, and games round out just some of what is available for the outdoor enthusiast. Much of it is free and most of the rest is reasonably priced with a star rating system that helps to quickly weed out lesser quality programs—three or four stars is my minimum.

A word of caution: these apps can be addictive. In my view, there is a secret to adding a smart phone as part of an arsenal of tools for enjoying the out-of-doors: make sure that its use enhances the experience and doesn't supplant it. If you aren't getting outdoors because you are spending so much time messing with your outdoor apps, you have missed the point.

Essentials

On a work assignment not long ago, I hiked up the steep hill and began to regret some of the weight I was packing. Between gasps of breath, I considered what I could have left behind. I started to laugh. I had no less than 5 electronic devices on my person: an FRS two-way radio, a second two-way radio with channels specific for work, a cell phone, a GPS and a PDA. If I could have brought it, my laptop computer would have been there too.

What was funny was that I couldn't see how I could function that day without any one of them. Funnier still, ten years ago, none of them would have been in my pack.

Hunters and fishermen are an especially peculiar breed of outdoorsmen. If you are one or you know one, you know what I am talking about. One of their greatest eccentricities is the absolute conviction that every new gadget that comes along is THE answer to all their hunting and fishing woes. They may lead all outdoor enthusiasts in money spent on doodads, devices, and contraptions to compensate for lack of skills in the field or to add another, bigger, smaller, stronger, or just different tool to the arsenal.

Then there is overkill. While hunting, a friend proudly showed me his knife. Then he showed me his other knife, and another until he had seven blades laid out with associated sheaths and sharpening stones. One was suitable for butchering an elephant; two looked like armament for gang warfare. I wasn't impressed as much by his knives as I was by his stamina. In my self-righteous state, I didn't even feel the weight of my own three knives (not counting my multi-tool, of course).

I know people on the other end of the spectrum as well. My friend, Dennis, endurance runs through the mountains for 40 miles carrying only water and energy packs, overtaking hikers burdened down with "survival essentials" and other equipment outdoor writers insist everyone should carry.

Surprising to me, two of my sons sit at opposite ends of the equipment continuum. One is a minimalist, hardly seeing the point of one knife, much less seven. For him, a couple of PB&J sandwiches, a few rounds for his rifle, and cotton jeans and he is good to go. My other son's day pack weighs more than a watermelon.

I determined to see what others carried in their daypacks, fanny packs and backpacks. Ostensibly, this was so I could smugly point out all the useless and ridiculous things that people carry. In reality though, I was looking for good ideas for things my pack might be missing.

Some of the lists I found read like Cabela's catalogs. Prepared for anything is an understatement. One fellow claimed to carry 500 feet of parachute cord. I don't think there is even that much on a real parachute. Lighters, Gore-Tex everything, survival kits that duplicated everything in their pack, extra socks, and enough ammo to start a war were all common themes.

I have a theory on why we carry so much. It is all part of the dream. We almost hope, even dare, nature to throw us a curve, force us to pull out that space blanket and hunker down to survive. We see ourselves beside a fire started with flint and steel, gnawing on roasted squirrel that was caught in a snare of our own making (why we would eat squirrel when our packs are stuffed with nutrition bars is not the question). Snow swirls around us, wolves howl, but we are smugly confident we will survive.

Darby Girls Camp

I spent last week at Darby Girls Camp. I wasn't a stalker; my role was to be a beast of burden, general fixit guy and gofer for my wife, who was camp director for the week, while keeping my male image in low profile. The girls practiced camping skills, shot bows and arrows, hiked, rappelled and learned about nature. Cellphones, iPods, and other electronics were strictly prohibited. The young ladies developed an enthusiasm for camping, a new experience for many.

This particular camp recently underwent a massive makeover, including an upgraded septic system, new restrooms and bear-proof storage at each campsite to be compliant with US Forest Service regulations. Forest Service regulations? Why should this camp be required to follow Forest Service regulations?

Like several camps in the area, including a YMCA camp, School District 93's Pine Basin, several Boy Scout camps and Camp Tamanawis, another girls camp, this camp is on Forest Service property. The buildings are owned by the various entities but they sit on property leased from the government.

Leasing property is nothing new for the Forest Service. Nationwide, there are over 14,000 private cabins on leased Forest Service lands. The Forest Service also leases property for ski resorts, lodges and other commercial ventures. In addition, partial leases for grazing, timber, oil and gas extraction, and mining are all part of the multiple use directive.

At 60 years old, Darby Girls Camp is well established, but it had a rough start. In its second year (1951), tragedy struck the camp when four girls and a leader were killed by lightning while on a hike to the wind cave in Darby Canyon. The camp and the program survived the incident though, and a little math indicates that over the course of nine weeks each summer, an average of 1200 girls and 600 leaders spend a week at camp. That makes 72,000 young ladies whose lifelong interest in nature may have started in Darby. Many of the women leaders there last week had attended Darby Girls Camp as teenagers and accompanied daughters and granddaughters that week.

It might be surprising to learn that there was a strong push to retire the lease for the camp several years ago. Some felt that the impacts created by having a concentration of humanity in a sensitive area were inappropriate. Others felt that the once-a-week hike day was affecting the wilderness quality of the surrounding area.

While the impacts are real, I may part company with some in the environmental/conservation community when I argue that there is no better use for the property that these camps occupy. My justification is simple: with the very real threat of Nature Deficit Disorder plaguing our children, the worst thing we can do is allow disinterest, apathy, and fear of nature overwhelm the next generation.

Darby, and other camps like it, offers a structured environment in which to introduce our youth to the working of nature beyond a television set. Kids can get dirty, learn to deal with the elements, and begin to appreciate a world beyond electronic gadgetry. When kids come to love and respect the natural world, it follows that they will want to take good care of it. That makes these camps invaluable to the resource and worth the cost.

Fifty Ways to Learn From Nature

The task: Create a nature hike that would entertain and teach a large group of young ladies. Location: Big Hole Mountains near Victor. I wasn't hot on the idea, but I had accepted the assignment. And now I was frustrated because stubborn snows and an early summer camp date ruled out the normal and more challenging hiking activities.

It was already mid-afternoon when Cathy and I shouldered our daypacks to scout a trail for later in the week. Rain had chased us from Idaho Falls to the trailhead, but at the moment it wasn't raining and there was even a hint of a break in the weather. We were headed for a high ridge and I briefly fretted about lightning. Oh well, if we died, others would know not to make the hike there.

As we started up the trail we puzzled on how to make this hike fun, interesting, and a learning experience. Heavy rain clouds sagged against the Tetons, obscuring the view. I groused. Cathy reminded me that just because we can't see something doesn't mean it isn't there. Hmmm. Borderline profound. An idea began to form as we hiked and talked.

Could we find fifty more object lessons and educational experiences in a three mile hike? Fifty sounded outrageously ambitious but we committed by starting with number fifty at the end of the trail and working backward.

Each obstacle, every plant became a potential lesson, As we observed and applied what we were seeing, Nature quietly and gently tutored us. We began to see lessons everywhere.

Cheatgrass, a pernicious invasive weed, became a lesson in allowing "weeds," like laziness, to overcome our lives and cheat us of the future we deserve.

A tree across the trail was a reminder that in life there are often obstacles between us and where we hope to go. Obstacles need to be stepped over, around or removed and sometimes this is difficult. The struggle strengthens us.

Rock cairns were a cue that sometimes the path we must follow is not easy to see and we must walk by faith from cairn to cairn. They stood as reminders that as we work out a difficult path, we should leave markers to make it easier for others to follow.

A wrong turn in the rain forced us to backtrack half a mile uphill. No problem: life is like that. We all follow rabbit trails and dead ends as we pursue goals. Recognize detours and get back on the trail as quickly as possible.

A large pile of pine needles marked the nest of a colony of red ants. Ants are a great reminder of what can be achieved when individuals each do their small part in a united common cause.

A beautiful larkspur flower deserved a mark. This plant joined dozens of other species to form a wildflower kaleidoscope of color. Yet, the larkspur harbors a deadly secret: beautiful as it is, it is poison to livestock. Indeed, beauty may only be skin deep, and we can all have a fatal attraction to colorful and exciting, but deadly temptations.

Muddy tracks and scat proved the existence of unseen elk, mule deer, and moose. Pocket gopher tailings signaled a world of activity beneath our feet. Unraveling their stories was like peeling the layers on an onion, each layer removed reveals another. Human relations require us to be able to "read sign" to understand what is going on, not at the surface but rather, deep in the emotions.

Whew! Within a few hundred yards of the trailhead, we planted the last flag, marking fifty lessons about life and Nature. And the best lesson of all: with a little thought, dedication, and determination, an obligation became a memorable experience—duty became joy.

Street Names

It must be hard to come up with creative street names. It is predictable that every major municipality takes an easy-out, offering a free geography lesson by naming streets after states. If the city is large enough, all fifty might be represented. And major cities are often included, perhaps as reminders of ancestral roots. Sure, that is more creative than numbers, but still lacking panache. A subdivision in my neighborhood may have hit new creative heights when the developers named the streets after their kids. Cute.

Sometimes new streets are named for wildlife. This is nothing original and it's hardly creative, but wild animals are an essential part of our culture and this is our way to bring it home every day. Who wouldn't want to live on Bluebird Lane or Caribou Drive as opposed to 5th Street?

But not every species gets a street. If that were the case, there would be more than enough names to go around. There aren't many Starling Roads, Norway Rat Circles, or House Mouse Highways. Lobsters and clams might make the grade because they are tasty, butterflies and honeybees because they are pretty or perform a service, but most other invertebrates are less charismatic and because of that, their names don't inspire. Clearly, you've got to be cool to become a street name.

That same rationale seems to hold true for extinct species. After all, what Dodo bird would name a street for a species that doesn't even exist anymore? Wouldn't that have the potential to jinx your entire neighborhood with the same fate?

At one time, it seemed that streets were named only for game animals. Names like pintail, deer, grouse, elk, mallard, bighorn, and moose have been perennial favorites and probably still dominate in the name game. However, as society has come to appreciate unhunted species, names like kestrel, lynx, tanager, badger, and ermine are gaining recognition. Still, names such as lizard, frog, toad, skunk, and shrew struggle for popularity, making one wonder how we could ever even consider electing a president named Newt (Gingrich).

This frenzy to find cool animal names seems to get carried away at times. It's silly to name streets for animals that don't even live in this part of the country. In Idaho, caribou is an acceptable stretch as we at least have caribou in the northern extremes of the state and had a character named Caribou Jack in the southern part. But you would have to go hundreds of miles east to see a cardinal, native bobwhite, or opossum, for example.

The dark side to naming streets after animals comes when we destroy their habitat for the privilege. I still have an ad from the Teton valley newspaper encouraging homeowners to buy and build on, "elk, deer, and moose winter range." Seriously. Surely they meant *former* winter range. Once houses are there, big game won't be welcome.

As partial mitigation, I propose that whenever we name a street in previously virgin habitat after an animal, the preceding or next street should have to complete the story. For example, Moose Lane might be preceded by a street named, Used to Be. Sharptail Road might be followed by, Gone but not Forgotten Street. One street before a subdivision road named Elk Ridge could be a street named, No More Lane.

Now, that's creative.

Religion on the River

Every time I step outdoors, I learn something new. Sometimes it is about nature itself. More often than not though, the lessons re-emphasize matters of character, reminding me of being in Sunday School.

A recent adventure to pursue the wily steelhead trout is a good example. During time spent making hundreds of casts, I had plenty of time to ponder what steelhead fishing teaches me about me.

Faith: Although generally viewed as a religious principle, no one needs faith more than the steelhead fisherman. Faith is required on two levels—first, believing that there are actually fish in the hole being fished—not a given with migrating steelhead—and second, that with enough casts, I will finally seduce one. The self-doubtful should stay home because the imponderable variables will drive you nuts. Am I casting too far? Not far enough? Using the right lure? Too much weight or not enough? Am I standing in the right spot? Location, location, location.

Steelhead faith is keeping your line wet even when you realize that *you* are part of the reason for a statistic of 12 hours per fish rather than two hours per fish.

Patience: Patience is an active verb for the steelhead fisherman. This isn't a sport where you wait for the salmon flies to hatch and then become dizzy from fighting fish. Steelhead fishing requires steadfast endurance: long hours standing on shore or belly deep in icy waters, rigging up time after time with fingers too numb to feel, without complaint. And most of all, it demands a line in the water at all times. You can't force it; all you can do is tolerate the suffering until you utter the magical words, "fish on!"

Vigilance: Daydreamers pay dearly when steelheading. "That's what you get for not paying attention," an angler across the river shouts as I miss my only strike (well, it could have been a snag) of the day. Eternal steelhead vigilance means never letting your mind wander, having faith in your technique, and patience to bear it all, just to be ready for that one strike.

Temperance: Steelhead fishing is often combat fishing, shoulder to shoulder in the best holes, each jockeying for the sweet spot, and the crowd isn't always friendly. Patience cracks as lines cross, and yet another fisherman, likely a foreigner from Boise, or worse, Salt Lake City, shoulders in, or the fisherman on my right or left becomes surly because I just did one of the above (or he saw my 8B license plate).

Steelhead temperance requires turning the other cheek when a fist to the nose is in order.

Charity: I know it sounds petty, but see that guy walking away with three steelhead on a stringer? I hope he rips his waders on the bushes. Steelhead charity would rejoice in the victories of others, but after a frustrating and futile day, charity isn't even in my vocabulary.

Faith wanes after long cold hours of fruitless casting. A bird's nest in the line on my reel mocks my vigilance. A snag, blessed for the short-lived spike in adrenaline when mistaken for a fish, is subsequently cursed as it robs yet another set-up and I am forced to rig up once again. Patience, in this case long-suffering, fails and the muttering under my breath becomes an uncharitable diatribe against anyone and anything steelhead.

Yes, fishing for steelhead becomes a great measure of how I have really progressed in development of my character, but it isn't something I'd report in Sunday School.

Teaching Kids About Nature

As a family, we have spent hundreds of nights tent-camped together (along with associated Scout and girls camps) as our children have been growing up. We tried the camp trailer thing but found that the convenience tended to remove us one more step from truly experiencing all camping had to offer. The more convenience we contrived to bring with us, the more we needed and we tolerated less disruption of our city lives. We were trying to "tame" the wilderness once again and force it to do things our way. After a short time, we sold the trailer and returned to the tent and an attempt to live with the natural world and not to conquer it. A lump or two under the sleeping bag or the occasional mosquito in the milk is just part of the experience.

Our children have loved the adventures we have had and we all look forward to our annual camping trip. We have made some concessions along the way, such as a solar shower (but even that is powered naturally) and a large propane grill, but still we strive for naturalness. Once, for example, I helped the boys make willow stick fishing poles, find natural bait, and with this minimalist gear, catch supper from a small creek. Another time, we practiced starting campfires with a magnifying glass. We have also eaten wild onions and slept in shelters of our own creation.

One of the most important lessons we learned, and this has been verified by experts, is that a child's view of the world is literally very different from that of an adult. Think for a moment about hiking with a child: while you are being filled with inspiration by the grand scenic vista before you, a child has been seeing nothing but bushes and dirt and perhaps eating a little dust from your boots. Their world consists of anything that is within three feet of the ground. If you cannot make that world interesting, they will become bored very quickly.

So, to bring a lot of excitement to the world kids see, get on their level. Pay attention to their squeals of delight; stop what you are doing and get down and dirty with them. I mean this literally. Nothing tells a child that he or his discovery is important better than having an adult get on his hands and knees and pay real and honest attention to it. This is not always easy advice to follow. I have been dragged, kicking and screaming, more than once from my comfortable hammock to look at any number of strange things from a hairy caterpillar to sculpin finning in a creek.

With each discovery, we sit down and play at "wondering". We try to hypothesize about the subject in hand. A child's questions can really provoke a learning session. I never have regretted the times I was moved to get down with the kids and really look at what was going on beneath my own observation zone. Their discoveries have often been the highlights of the trip.

A box full of various field guides, stargazers, handbooks (Boy Scout handbooks and field books are great references and are written for kids) and tools help us observe and teach. Even at a fairly early age, we have provided our kids with their very own binoculars and a magnifying glass. Yes, several have been lost or destroyed, but it has been worth it. Before each trip we remind the kids to bring them along. The books help to provide answers to questions such as: What kind of butterfly is that? Why can birds fly? Does a worm feel pain? The kids are armed with the tools to help them explore their world and everyone is equipped to check out the deer in the meadow or the moose at the far edge of the pond at the same time.

Parents who fail to prepare well for a camping trip risk disaster. But, with proper planning, taking kids camping will be a rewarding experience and can build a lifetime of memories, increased self-sufficiency, and instill a love of nature.

Backyard Habitat

It finally arrived. The recognition I had been waiting for and working toward for five years came in a plain white 9x12 envelope. My backyard, while still a work in progress, had been accepted by the National Wildlife Federation as true backyard habitat and I now have a sign and a certificate to prove it. I couldn't be more proud.

The National Wildlife Federation's Backyard Wildlife Habitat program was started in 1973. It was intended to encourage people to start thinking of their backyards as habitat rather than sterile manicured landscapes. This program has been consistently growing and by 2012, 150,000 backyards have received certification.

I was a bit surprised when I went to fill out the application to find that this was not a "give away" program, where anyone who asked could get certified. In fact, a backyard has to provide the basic habitat elements for wildlife, including food, water, and shelter, and it may take some concerted effort to get a backyard ready to qualify.

These basics can be provided in a number of ways from native plants to bird feeders and nest boxes, but they must be there. The backyard also must use some sustainable forms of landscape practices, such as composting, mulching, restoring native plants, and/or reducing chemical pesticides and fertilizers.

In my yard, I compost, mulch, and use drip irrigation to reduce waste and conserve water. While all my plants are not native, I do strive to use natives whenever I can find them and get them to grow. Water is supplied via a bird bath although a pond or stream is still in the plan. Spruce trees provide dense nesting habitat and I offer several nest boxes as well. Although there are a number of seed and berry-producing plants, including chokecherry, currant, skunkbush, cranberry, Siberian peashrub, and sunflowers, I still hang and fill feeders. As my yard matures and I continue to add wildlife amenities, I will apply for advanced certification.

It is easy to see if your backyard qualifies for certification or to get ideas and suggestions to build a backyard that qualifies. The first step is to log onto **http://www.nwf.org/backyard/** and go to the online certification link. I found that it was handy to print off the application so I would have a guide while building my backyard.

When your backyard qualifies it will cost only $20 to complete the certification process. This entitles you to a certificate, a one year membership with the NWF, a quarterly newsletter, *Habitat*, and a one year subscription to the award winning magazine, *National Wildlife.* If you want the sign for your backyard, it will cost an additional $25.

As open space is gobbled up by housing and commercial developments at a dizzying pace, it is obvious why everyone should take an interest in providing habitat for wildlife. Granted, this program won't replace what is being lost. And it certainly is no substitute for appropriate county planning, but it is a start. It also helps to realize that there is something that you or I can do on a personal level, with our own little slice of heaven, to help conserve wildlife. Any positive action is better than inaction.

It doesn't matter where you live or how small your yard or garden space is, it can be certified as wildlife habitat. I hope you will join me, Backyard Habitat #66575, in the quest to share our backyards with as much wildlife as we can.

One Hundred Ways to Die

Despite the recent spate of grizzlies behaving badly (from our standpoint), fatal animal attacks are very rare in comparison to other ways to die in our National Parks. Of course, a fundamental and frightening difference between animal attacks and other accidents in the National Parks is that the animals can bring the fight to you. Get too close, come between a mother and her young, or stumble past a food source, and trouble comes on the run.

But an animal might also back off or false charge, change its mind or become distracted by pepper spray. Not so a raging river or an avalanche. For instance, Yosemite National Park, a park with no grizzlies, bison, wolves, or moose, leads the nation in annual deaths. Ten to fifteen people die in the park each year, mostly from drowning and falls, and 2011 set a new record, with seventeen deaths by the end of August.

We need but look in the mirror to find the consistently most dangerous animal in the national parks. Yellowstone National Park averages around 500 vehicle accidents a year including several fatalities. Grand Teton, Everglades, Great Smoky—name the park, it will have similar statistics.

Although there are grizzlies, black bears, moose, and bison in Grand Teton National Park, they should fear us and not vice versa when we're behind the wheel. They are all victims in the nearly 150 vehicle/animal collisions a year in the park. These accidents almost always prove fatal to the animal and can be dangerous to the humans as well.

Falls, not bears, take the grisly fatal lead in Alaska's Denali National Park which saw its first fatal grizzly attack in 2012. In fact, there are many parks where falls are real killers. Some falls occur during expert mountaineering trips, but many are just your average tourist on a hike or someone trying to get that unique photo angle.

Glacier National Park is also known for its bears—but drowning, not wildlife, has a dramatic lead over other causes of death there. And nearly every park or recreation area reports a drowning or more each year. Yellowstone National Park adds thermal pools to the water hazards. They have claimed 20 lives, the latest as recently as 2006.

Yet the parks really are safer than this might make them seem. Even Yosemite, with well over four million visitors, has a fatality rate that equates to only 0.000004 percent of the visitors, hardly making it a hotbed of danger.

In fact, Yellowstone and Grand Teton Parks do not even make the top five of the most likely places to die on federal ground. Those honors go to, in order: Yosemite NP, Denali NP, Lake Mead National Recreation Area, Grand Canyon NP, and the Blue Ridge National Parkway.

Rangers are also quick to point out that in the vast majority of fatal or injury accidents in the parks, someone didn't use common sense, was unprepared, ignored warning signs, went around barriers, or disregarded the rules. The first fatality in Yosemite NP in 2013 was a young man who ignored warning signs and entered a swift river, only to be swept over the falls. From that perspective, dying in a park is almost a choice.

Avalanches, lightning, falling rock, raging waters, falls, vehicle accidents, or wild animals-- there are a hundred ways to die, even in a park. Nature should never be taken for granted regardless of where you are, but common sense and preparedness will get you safely back home.

CHAPTER SIX

LAST WORD

Bloom Where You're Planted

Along the Madison River inside Yellowstone National Park is a tree. This is not just any tree, although it is a lodgepole pine like most of the species in the area. It is unique not in what it is, but where it is. I have been watching this particular tree for about 20 years. And in 20 years it hasn't seemed to change much. It is still no taller than my waist, twisted, and of late showing signs of decline. This tree resides in the river, perched on top of a boulder where nothing is supposed to grow.

This tree didn't know that. Somehow, the seed from which it emerged found its way onto that rock. It could have fallen directly from its mother tree, swirled in on a breeze or floated in on high water. Or, perhaps a bird carried the seed there, building a cache for later use. Regardless, the seed was there, wedged in a small crevice where water could collect and initiate the germination process. Had the seed fallen upon the fertile deep soils along the banks there was genetic promise to be a giant. But the seedling took root in circumstances that would forever thwart that potential.

When I first saw this little tree 20 years ago, it was already established on the rock. I may never know its true age but I can imagine the annual growth rings crowded so closely together that they may appear as one. Growth sacrificed on the altar of survival.

Each day the tree is in a slow and relentless struggle, root against rock. Root tips probe into the fissures searching to exploit even the tiniest weakness. As water and root action erode nutrients from the rock, the tree absorbs what little there is; never enough to thrive, just enough to survive.

But something special is happening as the roots extend downward, perhaps only a few inches a year, and slowly add to their girth. They become a living wedge, one that eventually may split the resistant rock in two, exposing more of it to weathering and hastening its passage into soil, benefitting future generations of trees.

Thwarted by circumstance, this tree could not become the giant of its destiny. Potential is often moderated by reality. But the tree still struggled on and became a different but still necessary force in nature.

Whenever I see this tree, I think of my friend. With the genetic potential to be a football hero, an injury during birth left him unable to walk, every joint twisted and stiff. He struggled for how he could contribute and support himself.

Rather than dwell on what could not be, he played the hand he was dealt and became a successful draftsman.

Sometimes life is tough. Sometimes we land on the rocks or in the weeds, on our backs, or even on our heads. What matters though, isn't how we got there or what we could have done if the battering waves had been smaller, or if the sun would have shined on us, or if we had only settled on good soil. What matters is how well we do under the circumstances we are in-- how well we bloom wherever we are planted.

ABOUT THE AUTHOR

Terry R. Thomas and his wife, Cathy, are the parents of five children and grandparents of 10. They live in Idaho Falls, Idaho, where Terry writes a weekly Nature column for the Idaho Falls Post Register. He has been writing this column for 16 years. He writes on a wide variety of topics including humorous glimpses of nature, philosophy, and biology.

Terry is a professional wildlife biologist and has worked for Idaho Department of Fish and Game for 27 years. He began his career as a conservation officer in north-central Idaho. Later, he managed Tex Creek Wildlife Management Area for many years. He currently supervises the habitat program in the Upper Snake Region.

What Readers are Saying about NATURE

Your recent column, The Eyes Have It, was really wonderful. I frequently send your column off to friends around the West and it is always well received. This one, in particular, was very popular. Friends, and friends of friends (your columns get passed on and on down the internet line), are asking where to read your column.
Stephanie Smith

WOW. What a phenomenal piece you wrote. You are amazing.
Jennifer Jackson

I love reading articles that you have written. They are so down to earth, easy to understand, and keep your attention. It makes a person want to know what you are going to write about next, or when you will have an update article. Keep up the good work!
Cathy Kopke

LOVED your Lessons of Birds on Getting Along – have enjoyed your other articles too, just haven't sent a note.
Mary Terra Berns

Just wanted to tell you I appreciate the articles you have been writing. This one, Habitat Piranhas, particularly made me smile. Thanks - and keep 'em coming!
Leona Svancara

Editor: I also wanted to tell you how much I value Terry Thomas and his columns. They are wonderful!! They are well written and well reflect the wonder of Idaho's wildlife and nature. My thanks to him. I take great pleasure in reading them on-line each week.
J. Kent Marlor

I just read your latest nature column on the Power of One. Excellent! I always find your columns thought-provoking. Keep it up.
Bret Stansberry

Your article today was excellent as was the one a few weeks ago about your children becoming independent and moving out on their own. Excellent writing!
Lou Griffin

You hit a home run with your article on <u>Big Questions in Nature</u>. It should be required reading for all of our adults in this state who have lost touch with Nature......great job!
Joe Chapman

I just wanted to let you know that I really enjoy reading your articles in the Post. Thanks!
Lori Adams

Wanted to tell you how much we enjoyed your column last week, <u>Bloom Where Planted</u>. Some of your best writing yet. The Post Register is fortunate to have your weekly columns. This time I cut it out ---- often times my wife does it.
Lou Griffin

Great article in the paper. It's those special personal encounters with wild creatures that mean so much to us over the long term and they enrich our lives. Memories of those feelings---I remember the incredibly delightful feeling of a chickadee landing on the brim of my hat one frigid day in Antelope Creek, twenty-five years ago. Thanks for your story.
Ed Bottum

Made in the USA
San Bernardino, CA
07 December 2013